DREAMS
— AND —
VISIONS

GRAHAM FITZPATRICK
Author of
How to Recognise God's Voice

Sovereign World Ltd
PO Box 777
Tonbridge
Kent TN11 9XT
England

ISBN: 1 85240 057 9

Copyright© 1991 SPIRITUAL GROWTH PUBLICATIONS
P. O. Box 228, Fairy Meadow, 2519, AUSTRALIA

Edited by Shirley G. Spencer, Oklahoma, U.S.A.

Printed in England by Clays Ltd, St Ives plc.

Contents

Introduction

Dreams and visions are two supernatural ways God speaks to people. The Scriptures record that God has employed these means to reveal future events to people. He used a dream to rescue a godly man's wife from being forced to perform sexual intercourse with another man (see Genesis 20:1-18).

God used a vision to reveal to an old man that his barren wife would bear a son miraculously (see Genesis 15:1-17). By means of a dream He protected a man from the wicked intentions of his father-in-law (see Genesis 31:24).

A God-given vision led a violent religious hypocrite to be converted to Jesus Christ (see Acts 9:1-7). A dream saved a man, his wife and a son from being murdered (see Matthew 2:13-15).

God guided an old man to another country by a vision (see Genesis 46:2-4).

Besides these, many other dreams and visions are recorded in Scripture.

Nowhere does Scripture state that God ceased speaking to people through dreams and visions. Therefore, if the possibility exists that He may speak to us in these ways, we need to understand what the Word teaches about dreams and visions.

In the following chapters, we will learn how to distinguish between visions that come from God, those that come from human imagination and those originating with Satan. The difference between God-given dreams, natural dreams and other types of dreams also will be discussed.

We will consider the godly use of the human imagination. We will examine the idea that the more time and energy one devotes to seeking after supernatural dreams and visions, the more frequently God will give them. We also will examine the related question of whether He will grant us a supernatural dream or vision each time we ask for one.

The idea that all Christians can become "seers" also will be considered.

My prayer is that your relationship with God will be enriched by what you read here.

1
Two Extremes

Some church people claim that God no longer speaks through supernatural dreams and visions. They say that He spoke only to the Apostles in supernatural dreams, visions, and by angelic appearances.

This claim, however, is not in agreement with Scripture. According to Acts 9:10-16, God instructed Ananias by means of a supernatural vision. Ananias was not an apostle. The Scriptures do not say whether Ananias was even a church leader. He may have been a lay person. But Acts 9:10 does say he was a disciple.

A similar false claim is the idea that God gives dreams and visions only to His Prophets, Apostles, and the most holy Christians. This belief, also, is contrary to biblical account. Judges 7:13-15 records that God gave a dream to a pagan Midianite. According to Daniel 5:1-31, God spoke to a wicked pagan king by means of a vision. Genesis 41:1-7 reveals that God gave two dreams to a pagan Egyptian Pharaoh who believed in consulting satanic magicians and occultists (see Genesis 41:8).

The other extreme is evidenced when some church-goers overemphasize dreams and visions. Many of these people make dreams and visions into an *end in themselves*.

Dreams and visions should be regarded instead as a *means to achieving two aims*: (1) knowing Jesus Christ intimately and loving Him more than any other person or thing, and (2) doing His will daily.

The Apostle Paul emphasized the first purpose—knowing Jesus Christ—in Philippians 3:8:

> ...*I consider* **everything a loss** *compared to the surpassing greatness of* **knowing Christ Jesus my Lord**, *for whose sake I have lost all things.* . . .
> *(New International Version, bold type added)*

The other purpose is expressed by the Lord Jesus in John 14:15:

> *If you love me, you will* **obey** *what I command.*
> *(New International Version, bold type added)*

In the matter of supernatural manifestations, we should aim at the above two goals, not at receiving four-hour cinemascope visions and dreams each day in our prayer closet. If God chooses to reveal His purpose through dreams or visions, good. But let us be careful not to make the manifestations more important than knowing and loving Him.

Experiences Used Only as Examples

In later chapters of this book we will examine some spiritual experiences of people who received supernatural dreams and visions. These experiences, especially my own, are not quoted as an authority or basis of teaching and doctrine. A Christian must rely solely upon the Holy Scriptures as an authority for what he believes and teaches.

The focal point of this book is the Scriptures quoted and the explanations of these passages. Experiences or testimonies which relate to the author are given only as contemporary examples of truths which the Holy Bible already teaches.

It is important that we experience God and His love, power, forgiveness, cleansing and other miracles. It is insufficient to know only the correct doctrines of Christianity. Even though God is a God of truth (see 1 John 5:6; John 14:6), He is also a God who commands us to know Him in our daily experiences of life. Ephesians 3:19 shows this:

> (That you may really come) to know—practically, through experience for yourselves—the love of Christ, which far surpasses **mere knowledge** (without experience); that you may be filled (through all your being) unto all the fullness of God—(that is) may have the richest measure of the divine Presence, and become a body wholly filled and flooded with God Himself!
>
> (Amplified Version, bold type added)

We, however, cannot form our doctrines on the basis of our varying human spiritual experiences. Even some godly Christians over the centuries were deceived by spiritual experiences which suggested things contrary to the Holy Scriptures. God has provided the Bible as the final judge of true doctrine.

In writing this book, I wish to encourage you to keep **Scripture-based** teachings as the basis of your beliefs. Do not fall into the trap of forming your theology on your own or another's spiritual experiences, no matter how holy or dedicated to God you or he may seem to be.

2
God-Given Visions

The word *vision* has at least four meanings in English.

First, there is the biblical type of vision. These are given as God the Holy Spirit decides and wills, not in proportion to how much we desire or *seek after them*.

Examples of this type of vision are found in the lives of Ananias (see Acts 9:10-16), Peter (see Acts 10:9-16), and Ezekiel (see Ezekiel 1:1; 8:1-18).

In each of these instances, we see no evidence that before having these experiences, Ananias, Peter or Ezekiel were seeking for or expecting God to give them a vision or a dream.

Basically three categories of God-given supernatural visions are identified in Scripture. The first of these takes place when the receiver is given the ability to see the spiritual world and the physical world briefly at the same time. On such occurrences, the person's physical eyesight and other senses are not suspended. Examples of this phenomenon can be found in Judges 13:9-22 and 2 Kings 6:16-17.

The second category of biblical supernatural visions is identified in 2 Corinthians 12:1-4, where God suspended the person's physical senses for a short time, while enabling him to see the spirit realm.

In the third category of supernatural visions, instead of suspending the person's physical senses or revealing the spiritual realm through the person's physical eyes, God places a mere visual impression in the person's mind or spirit.

A Vision While Receiving the Holy Spirit

When a church elder prayed with me to receive the Holy Spirit, God gave me a vision. While I had my eyes closed, an incredible light appeared above my head. Though I could not see a face, I could sense the presence of Jesus Christ above me. Immediately, I felt compelled to bow myself as low as possible.

I did not see any of these things with my physical eyes. Nor did I go into a trance in which my physical senses were shut off (see Acts 10:9-16).

After being filled with the Holy Spirit, I went home. There I continued in prayer for hours. I confessed every sin that the Holy Spirit brought to my mind. I committed as many areas of my life to Him as I could think of. I was so filled with His presence that I felt that I was in heaven. When I looked out the window later at home, the moon appeared to be brighter then ever.

A Vision of North Africa

In October 1976, a visiting preacher came from another town. As he prayed with me, the Lord gave him a vision of North Africa, a jumbo jet and a particular number.

Since he knew nothing about me, he had no way of knowing that in the previous months of that year, the Lord had been speaking to me about going on a missionary journey to a specific country in North Africa. This vision was a *confirmation* of what God the Holy Spirit had been showing me. (Refer to chapter 10, "Other People's Dreams and Visions For Us," for more details on how God speaks to us through other people and the dangers involved.)

In 1981, I flew to a North African country on a jumbo jet, just as the Lord had revealed. My age at that time paralleled the particular number revealed in the visiting preacher's vision.

A Vision of Two Angels

Like most Christians I know, I have never seen a vision of an angel. But in 1974, God gave one of my mother's closest friends, Barbara Franks, a vision of two angels. The vision occurred at a week-night prayer service at her local church.

Barbara was seated at the back left-hand side of the church building. The leader's wife was praying for another woman at the altar area. Barbara also was praying for the woman, who seemed to have much unbelief blocking her relationship with God.

While Barbara prayed and looked at the woman being prayed for, she saw two angels flying close to one another horizontally across the front of the meeting. Barbara saw the angels with her eyes and not with her imagination. She had a full look at them, not just a fleeting glance.

They were not large angels. Their hair was relatively short and curly. Their long, soft garments, bodies and faces were all one color—a beautiful, life-filled beige color. Barbara was amazed at the shape of their soft-looking wings; they were more curved and thinner than she expected.

From the look on their faces, the angels apparently were very intent about the mission God had sent them on. The impression was one of intense speed. They did not look

13

at Barbara, nor did they say anything to her or anyone else.

Barbara was amazed by the angelic appearance. But while it was happening she had a great rejoicing and peace in her spirit. Later, she shared the vision with her leaders, who were greatly encouraged by this sign of God's working among them.

Overcoming Religious Tradition

In 1982, God gave a dream to one of my relatives to help her cope with the loss of her husband. He had been born-again a few years earlier and walked with God until his death.

Because she had been a member of a local church which taught many man-made traditions, she arranged for a church service to be held a week after his death. This service was for the purpose of praying her husband out of purgatory.

A few days after the death, God gave her a dream showing her that her husband was already in heaven. God gave her this dream to show her that in New Testament times, the dead go immediately to only two places—heaven or hell. God was also trying to save her unnecessary tears and worry about her husband's supposed sufferings in purgatory.

God is patient. Sometimes He will even send dreams to try to rid us of man-made religious traditions.

3
Godly Use of Imagination-Meditation Visions

The second type of vision, the godly use of human imagination-meditation-type visions occur when a Christian decides to mentally visualize the implications of some verse of Scripture.

With Psalm 91:2-4 as a basis, I may meditate upon a situation in which God protects me like a Roman fortress or like an eagle protecting its young. Upon reading these verses, another Christian may picture a situation in which God protects him like an English fortress in the Middle Ages, or like a hen protecting her chicks. Such "visions" are a result of *the human mind choosing* what to imagine after reading the particular passage.

If these were God-given, supernatural visions, such as those recorded in the Scriptures, the human mind would not be able to choose between different types of fortresses or birds. For example: Daniel 8:1-8 does not say that Daniel decided for himself what sorts of animals he was to see in his vision. God made that choice. Daniel was to see a ram and a goat in his vision.

Godly use of human imagination visions are different from those recorded in the Scriptures.

The Human Imagination in Scripture

The Sacred Scriptures speak about the human imagination. They emphasize especially how we tend to use our imaginations for evil purposes. For example, in Noah's time, Genesis 6:5 records:

> *And God saw that the wickedness of man was great in the earth, and that every imagination of the thoughts of his heart was only evil continually.* *(Authorized Version)*

Genesis 8:21 says:

> *. . .and the Lord said in his heart, I will not again curse the ground any more for man's sake; for the imagination of man's heart is evil from his youth. . . .*
> *(Authorized Version)*

In 1 Chronicles 29:18, David prayed:

> *O Lord God of Abraham, Isaac and of Israel, our fathers, keep this for ever in the imagination of the thoughts of the heart of thy people. . . .* *(Authorized Version)*

Acts 4:25 says:

> *Who by the mouth of thy servant David hast said, "Why did the heathen rage, and the people imagine vain things?"*
> *(Authorized Version)*

Note what Paul commands we should do with our imaginations:

> *Casting down imaginations, and every high thing that exalteth itself against the knowledge of God, and bringing into captivity every thought to the obedience of Christ. —*
> *2 Corinthians 10:5* *(Authorized Version)*

16

This verse says that we must *pull down* or demolish everything we imagine that elevates itself above the true knowledge of God. The true knowledge of God is centered in the Sacred Scriptures. Therefore, *any imagined thing* which is *contrary to the teachings of the Scriptures* is *evil* in God's estimation.

Note also that the word *meditate*, used in the original Hebrew (Joshua 1:8; Psalms 1:2; 19:14; 63:6; 77:12; and 143:5) means "to ponder, imagine, mutter, speak, study, talk and utter".[1] This reveals that one aspect of meditating on God's Word involves the use of one's God-given imagination.

Never forget, however, that Joshua 1:8, Psalms 1:2, 63:6, 77:12, and 143:5 emphasize meditating on God's Law, His Word, His works, and mighty deeds recorded in Sacred Scripture. Therefore, the use of the human imagination can only be termed "godly" if it is being used for purposes that are in total agreement with the teachings of the Holy Scriptures taken as a whole. Any use of the imagination for contrary purposes falls into the category of evil use spoken of in Genesis 6:5 and 8:21.

For example, there are many non-Christian books and courses which encourage people to picture themselves as millionaires, being married to a certain person they desire and obtaining whatever they want (without any consideration of God's will in any of these matters). They say that this imagining activates certain mental or spiritual forces which cause these goals to be fulfilled. This use of imagination is evil and has its roots in pagan Eastern religion and witchcraft. James 4:13-16 is one passage which reveals that such ignoring of God's will is very sinful.

FOOTNOTE:
1. James Strong, *Exhaustive Concordance of the Bible,* (Riverside Book and Bible House, Iowa Falls, USA).

Some Reject All
Uses of Human Imagination

Some Christians have rejected the use of the human imagination in the meditation of God's Word. They infer that it is wrong to imagine such things as Jesus' returning to Earth, according to the description given in Matthew 24:30-31, Acts 1:9-11, 1 Thessalonians 4:16-17, and Revelation 19:11-21. They claim it is wrong to imagine the Lord Jesus storming into the temple, throwing out the money changers, according to the description given in Luke 19:45-46.

But based on my previous definition of the Old Testament word, *meditate*, it is godly to use our imaginations to picture things which are in agreement with the words of the Scriptures.

When meditating on verses of Scripture regarding Jesus' return to Earth, it is impossible to envision exactly what His face looks like. No paintings or sculptures of Jesus exist that were produced while He was here on Earth. All paintings and sculptures of the Lord are *mere guesses* of what He looked like.

Try reading some of Jesus' parables without using the imagination to visualize what He said. Some of His parables speak of good and bad trees producing good and bad fruit (see Matthew 7:17-19); men building their houses on rock or sand and the rain, floods, and winds coming against these houses (see Matthew 7:24-27); seed being put in different types of soil (see Matthew 13:1-8); a net catching good and bad fish (see Matthew 13:47-50); and an owner of 100 sheep losing one, then searching for it until it is found (see Luke 15:1-7). It is impossible for most people to read these stories without using their imaginations to picture what is said.

Luke 8:9-10 reveals that without a revelation from God, no one can understand the spiritual truths Jesus spoke about in figurative language in His parables. A person can use his imagination to picture men building their houses on rock or sand; he can "see" the rain, floods, and winds beating against those houses (see Matthew 7:24-27), and yet not understand the parable unless the Holy Spirit reveals its meaning.

This passage of Scripture does not mean that Jesus only uses parables when speaking to those specific unbelievers to whom He does not wish to reveal spiritual truths. Such an interpretation of Luke 8:9-10 is wrong. Otherwise, it would mean that no believer should waste his time reading the parables, since Jesus will not speak to him through them.

The figurative language Jesus used in His parables illustrated the spiritual truths He spoke of literally.

When speaking of how to preach the gospel, the great 19th century evangelist Charles Finney said,

> Preaching should be parabolical. That is, illustrations should be constantly used, drawn from incidents real or supposed. Jesus Christ constantly illustrated His instructions in this way. He would either advance a principle and then illustrate it by a parable—that is, a short story of some event, real or imaginary—or else He would bring out the principle in the parable. . . .[2]

Be Cautious of
Some Counselling Techniques

All Christians should be wary of a certain use of the imagination employed by some churchgoing counsellors. With this technique the person being counselled is told

---

[2]Charles Finney, *Revival Lectures* (Fleming H. Revell Co., Old Tappan, New Jersey, U.S.A.) p. 234.

to close his eyes and picture himself going down under the sea and then stating what he sees there.

I experienced this method of counselling several years ago when my godly Christian counsellor, whom God used in many ways, began using this technique. I was asked whether I saw any treasure chests or skeletons or anything else. I was told that whatever I pictured symbolized something from which God wanted my subconscious mind to be released.

These vain imaginings were said to be visions from God. They were not. They were merely the fantasized concoctions of the human mind.

On an exceptional occasion, God could use this type of vain imaginings, just as He spoke once through a donkey (see Numbers 22:24-33).

Some psychiatrists show their patients unconventional pictures and ask them what they interpret these drawings to mean. Patients often claim to see all sorts of weird and wonderful things in these drawings. Other psychiatrists use a technique of stating various words and asking their patients to respond with the first thought that enters their minds.

These psychological techniques may reveal some hidden memories and therefore have some value. But to claim that these are Holy Spirit-inspired revelations would be equally as ridiculous.

These psychological techniques are *hit-or-miss natural* methods. They are *not infallible divine revelations*. A response of "aunty" to the word *mother* may mean that the person looked to his aunty as his mother when he was a child. The response "aunty" to the word *mother* by another patient may reflect the fact that the child felt that his aunty and his mother were exceptionally close when younger.

Likewise, picturing a treasure chest under the sea may

indicate a love of money in one person or an interest in reading pirate stories in another. Picturing a skeleton under the sea may mean that you hated your father, or you may have been to a funeral yesterday.

Some counsellors get themselves in all sorts of trouble by not distinguishing between natural testing methods and divine revelations.

A Second Category

A second category of imagination type visions is the godly use of those created in the human mind when God speaks to it by the inner voice of the Holy Spirit or by a specific promise in the Holy Scriptures.

For example, if the Holy Spirit speaks to a man the words, "Your wife is going to have a baby next year," the man's imagination may form a purely natural mental picture or vision of his wife, the baby, and the hospital. If God spoke the same words to another man, he may decide to mentally picture the baby at home in his arms. These are different mental pictures in response to the same revelation via the inner voice of the Holy Spirit.

This illustrates that such visions are not 100 percent creations of God, but are created by human imaginations responding in different ways to *words* put in them by God. Therefore, this type of vision is not the same as those spoken of in Scripture, but is a human creation resulting from the operation of the inner voice of the Holy Spirit in a person's mind.

An example of this is found in 1 Kings 17:2-6. God spoke to Elijah telling him that He had ordered some ravens to feed him at the ravine of Kerith. In response, Elijah trusted God to perform this miracle.

Note that God did not tell Elijah what specific type of food the ravens would bring. In response to God's

21

revelation, Elijah could have pictured himself being given figs or grapes. Or he could have envisioned himself being served olives. He could have thought of some type of vegetable. But as it turned out, the Lord commanded the ravens to supply Elijah with bread and meat. Note that the Scriptures do not call this revelation a "vision".

Often the Lord has put thoughts into my mind which have resulted in my creating a mental picture of what He said. For example, between 1976 and 1981, God revealed to me that it was His will I go on a missionary journey to a North African country. As a result, I began to form a mental picture of this occurring.

Some of the specific details of the pictures I formed in my mind were different from what God later revealed was His will. I saw myself staying in North Africa for many years. This, however, was my mind wrongly interpreting the inner guidance of the Holy Spirit, revealing the *fallible* nature of mental pictures or "visions" created by the human imagination in response to God's inner promptings.

Use in Exercising Faith

The godly use of human imagination can be used also as one means of expressing faith in God for a specific miracle. This practice, however, is only sanctioned by the Scriptures, if what we are choosing to picture mentally is something *God has revealed specifically is His will.*

Years ago, God the Holy Spirit showed me that He wanted me to write books for missionaries and church leaders, especially for those in countries where biblical teaching books are scarce. Part of my faith response to this revelation was to form a mental picture of this one day occurring. I did not dwell on this vision every minute of every day, but only occasionally.

When God reveals His will to us, we need to make sure that *our thoughts, imagination, words and actions* express that we *believe* that what He says will come to pass.

Note also that this use of the human imagination *does not earn* us a miracle. Nor does it force God to give us one. It is merely one aspect of a *faith response to God's revealed will.*

However, trying through mental picturing to force God to perform a specific miracle that He has not revealed as His will, either through His Scripture or by His Spirit, is *sinful presumption*. This use of the human imagination is not an expression of biblical faith but is *virtually an occultic practice*. Anyone involved in such activity needs to repent immediately. If they don't repent, they may come under the partial control of an evil spirit of witchcraft.

4
Fleshly Visions

Some visions are "goals" or "aims" that are merely *the creation of Christians' minds concentrating on their own will* and not God's will. These goals or aims or "visions" are products of the old, sinful, flesh nature and can be even Satan's suggestions. Isaiah 65:2 says: *"All day long I have held out my hands to an obstinate people, who walk in* **ways not good, pursuing** *their* **own imaginations**. . ." (N.I.V.).

I have heard many Christians quote verses of Scripture out of context, or contrary to the meaning of other parts of the Word, in order to suggest that God is obligated to grant them these goals or aims or "visions" if they pray enough, "believe" enough, praise enough, or do some other action. Such so-called "divine visions" are selfish attempts to manipulate the Lord of all glory.

A Rolls Royce

A few years ago, I attended a large Christian conference in Sydney, Australia. Several thousand people at the conference heard various overseas and local speakers. One of the speakers, an African evangelist, had been used greatly by God.

While preaching, this evangelist shared a vision he claimed to have had in which the Australian head of the conference received one or more Rolls Royces. The evangelist asked the crowd to pray, positively confessing and claiming these cars for the Australian director. This was supposedly the leader's "new creation rights," or "inheritance in Christ."

Later at the same conference, I heard this same preacher threaten his audience with God's judgment. He said that any listener who had $1,000 (Australian) or more in his bank account, and was unwilling to put it in the conference's offerings, probably would be judged by God.

Putting two and two together, anyone could see that the listeners with $1,000 or more would be indirectly providing the Australian leader unnecessarily with a Rolls Royce or two.

The African evangelist distorted the meaning of the expressions, "new creation rights," and "inheritance in Christ," and used them in ways contrary to that intended by the original, Holy Spirit-inspired biblical authors. His vision was a fleshly goal that would have disgusted the Apostles and Old Testament Prophets.

Many godly missionary groups, such as Open Doors with Brother Andrew, the Slavic Gospel Mission, and the Bible Societies could have used these thousands of dollars far better by providing Bibles and Christian literature for needy pastors in Communist/third world countries. Many of these pastors are fortunate to have even one Bible and one Christian book.

Something is seriously wrong when a preacher has a vision to use *other people's money* (not his own) to provide someone with an *unnecessary* luxury car, when the money could have been used for the real needs of God's church.

Owning a Rolls Royce is not a sin, if you buy it out of your own money, or if it is a gift, and you have some godly purpose for it. But it is very wrong to pressure Christians by threats of divine judgment in order to obtain offerings to buy one or more for a preacher friend.

Suppose the Apostle Paul had told his listeners that they must put most of their gold in the offering, then had them pray in Jesus' name claiming Emperor Nero's palace and his many servants as his own. Then later, word spreads around Rome that Paul bought Nero's palace and servants for his own pleasure out of the sacrificial offerings of God's people. What fuel for unbelievers to use to discourage others from becoming Christians!

When I preached in Malaysia a few years ago, local pastors confirmed my impressions. They told me of similar problems in money matters this same preacher had while holding a series of meetings there.

It is wrong to attempt to justify our own fleshly, unscriptural visions by claiming that they are God-given. Even worse is threatening God's judgment on those who will not help us fulfil such fleshly visions. This is especially true when one is a respected evangelist through whom God has performed great miracles.

It is also sad when Christians treat any preacher as an infallible superstar. Instead of comparing the preacher's word to the Scriptures taken as a whole, they gullibly accept all that he says. They imagine wrongly that success in ministry and many accompanying miracles means that God approves of all the clergyman preaches or does.

In some parts of the earth, the church suffers greatly because of preachers who claim to have all sorts of visions and revelations for their listeners, which are mere products of vivid human imagination. Some of them have true revelations from God mixed with many of their own vain imaginings.

Some of these promise to offer special prayers in exchange for large money donations. These preachers claim to know special prayer techniques which will release financial blessings to those who give them generous contributions. They infer, also wrongly, that they are God's favorites—a claim contrary to Romans 2:11, 2 Chronicles 19:7, Acts 10:34, and Ephesians 6:9. Some of them attract many followers because they appeal to the selfishness present in all humans—telling their listeners that God wishes to grant their every selfish whim and desire. No distinction between selfish cravings and what God regards as their real needs is given by such preachers.

Some preachers presently are *being dealt with by God* about their idol-worship of money, their twisting of various biblical verses to justify this idolatry, dishonesty about supposed revelations and the number of miracles in their ministries, bleeding God's people to pay for their own fleshly goals, and other sins. As Revelation 2:21 reveals, God gives people a period of time in which they can repent. During this period of grace on the person's ministry, God may continue to use the preacher to bring many people to Himself and as a vehicle of many wondrous miracles.

At the end of this period of grace, God may discipline him. Hebrews 12:5-11 speaks of God's discipline in New Testament times. He disciplines His children in order to help them not ruin their spiritual lives. Some preachers already have been disciplined by God for the good of themselves and the church.

Balaam is a prime biblical example of a spiritual leader who gradually destroyed himself and his ministry because of a sinful attitude to money (see 2 Peter 2:14-15, Jude 11, Revelation 2:14). Balaam was a prophet of God (see 2 Peter 2:15-16) and was used by God to proclaim many wonderful Holy Spirit revelations (see Numbers chapters 23 and 24). Note that Numbers 24:12-14 reveals that a God-called ministry can publicize that he will not do anything motivated by a wrong attitude to money while inwardly being enslaved to it.

Let us hope that many preachers who have fallen into

a love of money, dishonesty about the number of miracles in their ministry, etc., repent. The church worldwide needs its preachers to be free from such bondages.

Bringing Disgrace to the Gospel

There are a number of godly television preachers in the United States. But sadly, a number of them are bringing disgrace to the church because of their non-stop sales pitch for money. For every unbeliever that they lead to Jesus Christ, there are probably ten others who have become more hardened to the gospel and more cynical about churches as a result of these tele-evangelists' activities.

Some of these tele-evangelists send out all sorts of so-called "anointed" objects saying that if you send in a money donation, God will work through the "anointed" oil, cloth, sponges or whatever giving you almost whatever you want. The wording of such appeals for money are obscure so that one is not sure if it is the money given, and/or the prayer and faith of the evangelist and/or the prayer and faith of yourself and/or the anointed object which is "causing" God to grant your miracle.

The above practices of certain tele-evangelists indicate a certain amount of lack of faith on the preacher's part and have given unbelievers much ammunition with which to write off all churches as money-grabbing selfish institutions.

These tele-evangelists claim that their "anointed" cloths and so on are based on the Apostle Paul's practice mentioned in Acts 19:11-12. But note that Paul's anointed cloths were not accompanied by a request for an offering or a claim that such an offering would work together with prayer and faith to cause God to give you almost anything you want.

These latter tele-evangelists usually have very expensive

"worthwhile" projects that are the cornerstones of their appeals for money. But no project—no matter how seemingly godly—is worth giving the wonderful gospel of our Lord Jesus Christ and the local Bible-centered churches which feed and care for believers a bad name. Unbelievers are always looking for excuses to attack the gospel and God's churches. But Christians are fools to give unbelievers ready-made ammunition to do so.

Many tele-evangelists have a short memory. They have forgotten that one of the causes of the Reformation in the 16th century was the preaching of the scoundrel monk, Tetzel, who promised that money donations to the Church would buy the miraculous exit of one's relatives out of the so-called "fires of purgatory". These activities were justified because the money was "needed" for the "holy, worthwhile" purpose of building St. Peter's Basilica in Rome.

If Christian leaders cannot preach the gospel of salvation through television and the radio without having to add all sorts of medieval superstitions and a constant over-emphasis on money in order to "keep the ministry going," then it is time that these leaders find some other cheaper means to preach the gospel. Otherwise, we will end up with every Tom, Dick and Harry who has a fleshly goal to be famous and wealthy through having an international media ministry, knocking on unbelievers' doors and giving them magic charms which will provide them with the miracle they want if they return the appropriate "seed faith" offering and believe and confess according to some formula.

5
Satanic Visions

There are visions caused by satanic miracles (see Revelation 16:14).

Remember, Satan and his demons can disguise themselves in a supernatural vision to look like angels (see 2 Corinthians 11:14). Satan and his demons also can disguise themselves to look like Jesus Christ, Mary, the so-called "Saints," and others.

We should *never try to manipulate* God to give us a supernatural vision or to send us an angel or to speak to us in an audible voice. If we try to force God to speak to us in these ways, a demon might see what we are doing and seize the opportunity to trick us by pretending to be Jesus Christ or an angel, or by imitating God's voice.

Many people involved in the occult, witchcraft, channelling, ancestor-worship, spiritualism, voodoo and pagan Eastern religions have received miraculous visions caused by demons. In these visions, evil spirits appear in many different forms. Sometimes, they pretend to be friendly spirits. At other times, they reveal some aspects of their wicked natures. Demons provide these visions in order to gain more control over the recipients and their friends and families.

The Visions of Jeane Dixon

The occultist Jeane Dixon is a classic example of a person who has received a number of visions from satanic origin. She says that her revelations come by means of visions, a crystal ball, astrology, numerology, dreams, cards, E.S.P., mental telepathy and occultic finger touching. Her occult practices began in a meeting with a female gypsy when Jeane was eight years old.

Dixon mixes her occult-witchcraft with Christianity. She attends Mass each day. Also, she repeats the 23rd Psalm every morning. This Psalm begins with:

> *The Lord is my shepherd, I shall not want. He maketh me to lie down in green pastures: he leadeth me beside the still waters. He restoreth my soul: he leadeth me in the paths of righteousness for his name's sake. . . . (Authorized Version)*

Dixon claims that her revelations are from God and that she has a personal relationship to Him. Dixon claims that every evening she commits her previous day and future life to God. She has gained much popularity in the United States through her accurate predictions of a number of things. It is claimed that while she was kneeling in front of the statue of the Virgin Mary in St. Matthew's Cathedral, she received a vision which predicted the assassination of the American President in 1962. She did not name him, but this was to be President John F. Kennedy. Many gullible people forget that the prophet Moses stated in Deuteronomy 13:1-5 that false prophets can sometimes predict the future accurately.

Dixon has also made many false predictions. One of these was that Richard Nixon, not John F. Kennedy would win the 1960 Presidential election. Dixon made this prediction in April 1960 after looking into a crystal ball.

Another false prediction was that World War III would break out in 1958. Later, she wrongly predicted on May 7, 1966 that the Vietnam war would finish 90 days after then.

An example of one of the satanic visions Dixon had, occurred on February 5, 1962. On each of the three nights prior to this vision, she had weird miraculous things happen to the five lights on the crystal chandelier in her room. She was meditating each time these miracles occurred.

The vision that Dixon had on February 5th began with Queen Nefertiti and an Egyptian Pharoah stepping out of the bright rays of the sun. The Queen was carrying a baby. The Pharoah and the Queen held the baby out towards Dixon. Wonderful bright rays of light then came forth from the baby. Because of this glorious light, Dixon could no longer see the Pharoah. She then looked at the Queen departing.

When Dixon looked again at the baby, he had become a man. A small cross appeared above his head and grew larger. People from all religions, races and color came to *worship him*. They were all in unity.

Dixon stated that this vision meant that on February 5, 1962, a child was born who would unite all mankind into one new Christianity by the end of the 20th century. She said this male is to be the answer to the problems of the world and its prayers. He will solve the problem of war and restore peace to this world. In 1999, all people will understand the complete fulfillment of this vision, she claimed.

There are two main reasons we know this vision is from demonic origin. First, Dixon obtains her revelations by means which are contrary to the teachings of the Holy Scriptures. Through the words of His Holy Prophets and Apostles as recorded in verses such as Deuteronomy 18:9-12, 2 Kings 17:17, Ezekiel 13:20-23, Acts 8:9-13, 13:6-11,

16:16-18, 19:18-19, Revelation 21:8 and 22:15, we see that God regards all forms of occult, psychic phenomena and sorcery as being wicked and demon-inspired.

Secondly, her vision contains things that are contrary to the teachings of the Holy Prophets, Apostles and the Lord Jesus who command that only God—Father, Son and Holy Spirit are to be worshipped (see Exodus 34:14, Deuteronomy 6:13, Matthew 4:10, Isaiah 2:11, 17). Matthew 4:10 says:

> *Jesus said to him, "Away from me, Satan! For it is written 'Worship the Lord your God, and serve him **only**.' (N.I.V.)*

When God the Son returns to earth, He is going to come back as a fully grown man, not as a baby again. The Scriptures state that He will be seen returning in the skies with His angels (see Acts 1:9-11, Matthew 24:30-31, Luke 17:22-24, Revelation 1:7, 19:11-21). Jesus was not reborn as a human baby in 1962.

Dixon claims that God wants everyone to worship the man she saw in her vision. But when we compare this man to the writings of God's true Prophets and Apostles, we find that they speak of the same person as being the Antichrist (see 1 John 2:18), the Man of Lawlessness (see 2 Thessalonians 2:3-12), the beast with the ten horns and seven heads (see Revelation 13:1-10) or the little horn who boasts and who wages war against God's true people (see Daniel 7:20-25).

2 Thessalonians 2:1-4 speaks of the Antichrist whom Jeane Dixon says people from all religions and races will worship:

> *Concerning the coming of our Lord Jesus Christ and our being gathered to him, we ask you, brothers, not to become easily unsettled or alarmed by some prophecy, report or letter supposed to have come from us, saying that the day of the Lord has already come. Don't let anyone deceive you in any*

way, for that day will not come until the rebellion occurs and the man of lawlessness is revealed, the man doomed to destruction. He will oppose and will **exalt himself over everything that is called God** *or is* **worshipped***, so that he sets himself up in God's temple, proclaiming himself to be God. (N.I.V.)*

Revelation 13:5-8 prophecies about the Antichrist also:

.The beast was given a mouth to utter **proud** *words and blasphemies and to exercise his authority for forty-two months. He opened his mouth to blaspheme God, and to slander his name and his dwelling place and those who live in heaven. He was given power to make war against the saints and to conquer them. And he was given authority over every tribe, people, language and nation.* **All inhabitants** *of the earth will* **worship** *the beast—all whose names have not been written in the book of life belonging to the Lamb. . . . (N.I.V.)*

Taken together, Revelation 12:9 and 13:4 reveal that Satan is behind the worship of this man who will be the Antichrist.

The fact that Jeane Dixon is a regular churchgoer, says the 23rd Psalm each day to herself and claims to have a personal relationship to God, reveals how deceptive demons are. If we do not test visions by the Scriptures, we could end up an instrument of Satan just like Dixon is.

Concluding Comments

By not showing the differences between these four types of visions mentioned in the last four chapters, some church leaders have created much confusion for their listeners. We need to know the differences between these, if we wish to be controlled daily by the Holy Spirit.

35

6
God-Given Dreams

There are also different types of dreams.

First, there are God-given, supernatural dreams such as those mentioned in the Scriptures. When we study verses such as Genesis 28:10-16, Genesis 41:5-7, 1 Kings 3:5-15, and Job 33:15, we see these occur when we *sleep* or are *partially asleep*. Note, however, that these types of dreams have a *different quality* and *greater clarity* than natural sleep dreams.

I have experienced 10 supernatural dreams given by God. These all occurred when I was asleep or beginning to awaken. I did not follow any "search" formula or technique before being given these by God. These dreams involved God's giving me knowledge and guidance regarding His will.

Two Dreams Together

God gave me my first supernatural dream when I was unmarried and living with my mother.

In the dream God told me that He wanted my mother and me to move from the house where we were living at the time. At exactly the same time, God gave my mother the first supernatural dream she had ever had. (I will give you details of her dream later.) Imagine the improbability of these dreams occurring at exactly the same time to two people living together.

As soon as I received this God-given dream, I awoke and started toward my mother's bedroom to tell her the details of my dream. Incredibly, at the same moment, she awoke and started toward my bedroom to tell me the details of her dream. We met in the hallway which joined our rooms. As we shared what had happened, we were amazed at how God had given both of us a supernatural dream at precisely the same time.

In the following weeks, we considered what God had told us about moving. In the natural it seemed impossible that we could move. My mother was a widow with very little financial resources. She still owed much money on the government-built house in which we lived. I was of little help financially since I was at university at the time.

Such a situation, however, was possible to God the Father. When He gave me the dream, He knew that in the near future a series of events would occur that would make the move possible.

First, my grandmother died. After her death, my grandfather decided to purchase a flat in a retirement village and, upon the insistence of my uncle and aunt, to leave his house to my mother. My uncle and aunt and their spouses were given a small dividend from the later sale of my mother's house. But this small amount was nothing compared to the amount of money they forsook in their kindness towards my mother.

Only God could have foreseen my grandmother's death, my grandfather's move, and my uncle and aunt's loving-kindness towards my mother.

Testing the Dream

In a later chapter, "How To Test Dreams and Visions," we will discuss in detail the principles of testing whether or not a dream or vision is supernaturally given by God.

But briefly, let's comment on this dream.

First, its content did not counsel me to take any action contrary to the Scriptures.

Second, when I received it, the peace of the Holy Spirit was present. While praying in the months following, I continued to sense a peace in my spirit from the Holy Spirit about our move.

Third, the action the dream foretold came to pass.

Get a Stronger Faith

In my mother's dream, the Lord instructed her that she needed a stronger faith because of all the troubles that soon would be coming into her life. What God told her transpired shortly afterwards. She faced more crises in a short time than she had confronted for many years, not the least of which was the death of her mother. Six months later her father also died; a grandson was told that he had leukemia (God later healed him); her dog was hit by a car, suffered for weeks, and then died; and her daughters had some terrible difficulties.

Before being bombarded by so many problems, my mother obeyed God's guidance provided in the dream. She developed a stronger faith in Him and His goodness, power and wisdom. She accomplished this by deepening her prayer life, meditating more on God's Holy Scriptures, and by daily committing her mind and body more to His control.

The Greatest Counsellor

Since the age of nine or ten years, I had battled with a number of problems in my own life. These disturbances were caused by several unconfessed sins that had begun in my life about that time.

While I was at university, I studied psychology, but these

courses did little to solve my problems. In my teenage years, I had asked many others about how to solve my problems, which provided some help.

It was, however, only after I recommitted my life to Jesus Christ at the age of 20 that I was able to understand the basic causes of these problems. By trusting God to speak to me, I was able to recognize the sources of these unresolved issues.

God is an infinitely greater Counsellor than any psychologist or psychiatrist. Over a period of years He revealed to me the root causes of each of my problems. He spoke to me in many different ways, one of which was supernatural dreams.

In one of these dreams, the Lord Jesus showed me a television screen-like picture of one of the sins in which I had been involved at ages 10 and 11. While showing me these things, He said, "This is it! This is it!" indicating that it was from this sin that my other main problems had developed.

In another dream He spoke the words, "willful disobedience," relating to a specific sin He revealed in the same dream.

In a third supernatural dream, I was given a television-like picture of myself being confronted with the temptation toward a specific sin into which I had fallen as a child. God repeated that dream on several occasions.

At first in the dream I could see myself being lured toward the sin. Then, I would say to myself, "No, God does not want me to do this." I would then pull away. Finally, though, I would allow myself to be enticed by the sin to the point of surrender. Then a terrible fear of God's rejection would overwhelm my mind.

In a fourth dream, the Lord Jesus revealed how I had allowed one of my mother's character flaws to become a part of my thinking also. He showed me a movie-like scene of my mother standing on a stage before a group of people. As she stood there, she began to feel embarrassed and rejected. The people began to laugh at her. Her face then turned a deep shade of red, and she looked even more rejected.

In the dream, I was watching this happen from a distance. But as my mother responded, I could feel myself sympathizing with her so intensely that I could sense her feelings of rejection being transferred to my mind.

This is exactly what happened to me as a child. As the youngest child—born many years after my two sisters—I was like an only child and was exceptionally close to my mother. I shared her feelings. As a small child I felt greatly loved and accepted. But as I grew older I became aware that my mother suffered much from thoughts of rejection, self-condemnation and similar attitudes. My child's mind came to incorporate into my thinking some of my mother's inappropriate attitudes.

The revelations of root causes of problems in my life did not necessarily provide their immediate solution. Only after confession, repentance and yielding to God was I able, with the help of the Holy Spirit, to break free over a period of time from these sinful attitudes. Even after many years, I must guard my mind from yielding again to these sins.

Jesus is truly the Wonderful Counsellor (see Isaiah 9:6). He not only revealed to me the root of my problems, in two other dreams He showed me how to pray in order to rid myself of some of the serious side effects of one of these sins. These two dreams occurred on two successive days just before I would awaken.

Romans 8:26 promises that God the Holy Spirit would help us know how to pray:

> *In the same way, the Spirit helps us in our weakness. We do not know what we ought to pray, but the Spirit himself intercedes for us with groans that words cannot express. (NIV)*

Ministering to Roman Catholics

God sometimes gives dreams that need to be interpreted in order to be properly understood (see Genesis 40:1-23; 41:1-40; Daniel 2:1-45; 4:1-27; 5:1-29).

Many years ago, I had a God-given dream in which I saw a local Roman Catholic church. I did not understand the meaning of the dream, yet it possessed a supernatural clarity and an intense presence of God.

I prayed for many months asking the Lord for the interpretation of the dream. The more I prayed about it, the more I received a deep Holy Spirit-inspired impression that God wanted me to minister to Roman Catholics in future years.

These impressions were not contrary to the Scriptures. Plus I often had an inner witness of the Holy Spirit confirming that these thoughts were from God.

Associated with the dream was God's later direction in my life. He led me to study church history at university and at a theological college. These classes concentrated on Roman Catholicism and early Protestantism. The Lord also led me into much personal study of Catholicism, Orthodoxy and Protestantism in the following years. The Lord also put me in contact with many individual Catholics who unknowingly helped me understand their teachings.

In recent years, God has begun to fulfil that impression He gave me regarding ministering to Roman Catholics. Thousands of copies of my book, *How To Recognize God's Voice*, have been read by Catholics in one Asian country. Catholics from other countries have written requesting copies of my books or asking for answers to various questions.[1]

---

[1]Do not take my comments here to mean that I believe in the joining together, organizationally, of all Protestants, Roman Catholics and Orthodox in one church. One of the reasons I am against such is because some denominations contain millions of

Another thing which relates to this dream is the many contacts that I have had with Catholic Charismatics over the last 13 years. I have developed a deep love and appreciation for these people. I have come in contact with them while preaching, at large conferences and in my local city. I know that they are pressured by non-Charismatic Roman Catholic clergy and lay people to accept certain man-made traditions and religious bondages. They are always in danger of being excommunicated by the Pope if they do not accept these unscriptural traditions.

Despite their problems in these areas, I have found many of them to be fine Christians. I believe that as many of them grow in Christ, they will obtain Holy Spirit-inspired wisdom which will lead them to abandon these man-made traditions.

An example of an unscriptural man-made practice is this: Some Catholic Charismatics imagine Mary coming in spirit form to hug them, if they have lacked parental love. But Mary is *not omnipresent*. She is not like God who can be present everywhere at the same time. She cannot appear in many different places on earth at the same moment, hugging many different people who might ask her to do so. To infer that Mary has an attribute that

---

"Christianized" pagans who try to dominate the more Jesus-centered, Holy Spirit-centered, Scripture-centered, godly members of their denominations.

What happens in the World Council of Churches is an example of this. There, the views of Charismatic, Evangelical and Pentecostal members are mostly pushed aside or watered down by spiritually dead liberal/modernist Protestants, tradition-centered Protestants and others. Imagine John the Baptist or the Apostle Paul's reaction to the suggestion that they should join together with the Jewish High Priests Caiaphas and Annas, and with the Pharisees because God supposedly "always hates disunity".

Many of the clergy in some denominations are Christian in name only. They are wolves in sheep's clothing (see Acts 20:29-31), unbelievers masquerading as followers of Jesus. According to 2 Corinthians 6:14-18, we cannot join spiritually with such people. We should love and minister to them, but not unite with them in local churches.

I believe in the uniting "in the Spirit" (see Ephesians 4:3) of all truly born-again Orthodox, Catholics and Protestants. This is different from organizational unity with many churchgoers who are not really a part of Christ's body.

In fact, born-again Catholics, Orthodox and Protestants likely will be persecuted much in the future by the many "Christianized" pagans in their own churches.

only God has—being able to be present at more than one place at a time—is very wrong. Many do this in ignorance, but it is still wrong.

Sports Equipment and a Dog

A lady counsellor, who later became a good friend of my mother, was given a number of dreams and visions from God. This lady often prayed for me.

On one occasion, the Lord gave her a dream in which she saw me holding various pieces of sporting equipment above my head. She said that God revealed to her that the dream symbolized that I had been making an idol of various sports.

In 1 Timothy 4:8 God reveals through the Apostle Paul that sports and physical exercise are of value in God's eyes, but walking with Him is more important:

> For physical training is of some value, but godliness has value for all things, holding promise for both the present life and the life to come. (NIV)

I had reversed the order and had made sports to be more important to me than my relationship with God. This was a form of idolatry.

I accepted this dream as being from God because it did not speak contrary to Scripture and because in the months that followed, the Holy Spirit *confirmed* to me that I had been making an idol of various sports: soccer, cricket, basketball, sprinting, and rugby league.

In her dream, my mother's friend also saw a small black dog. As soon as she mentioned the animal, I knew immediately what it meant. As a young man, between the ages of about 9 to 18 years, I had owned a small black dog. Caring for a pet is not sinful. I, however, had not only loved the dog, I allowed it to become an idol—more important to me than God. I confessed this sin.

I believe the Lord gave this dream so I would know what I needed to repent of and what to avoid in the future.

7
Other Types of Dreams

There are other types of dreams:

Human Imagination-Meditation Dreams

Some so-called "dreams" can be formed by our awake human minds after the Holy Spirit has put His words into them.

This type of dream does not correspond with the supernatural dreams mentioned in the Scriptures. This second type of dream is the same as the second type of vision mentioned earlier in that it is created by the human imagination responding to the inner still small voice of the Holy Spirit. Therefore, the words *dream* and *vision* in this category mean the same thing.

When we use the word *dreaming* to refer to the ability of our human minds to picture or imagine in faith what God has revealed is His will to perform, we are not using this word the way it is used in the Scriptures.

Fleshly Dreams

Some so-called "dreams" occur when we are not asleep and are merely the result of our human imaginations. Such dreams are not the result of the Holy Spirit's putting words into our minds. Such dreams are merely expressions of our fleshly "goals" or "aims". These are the same as the third type of vision mentioned previously.

Several examples of this type of dreaming have occurred in my life. I recall one instance when I had a "dream" or "goal" to travel in ministry regularly in part of the 1980's with a particular godly friend. My desire was so intense that I thought mistakenly that this was a God-given goal. God revealed to me later that it was not His plan.

Natural Dreams

Every human being has natural dreams which occur during sleep or when he is partially sleeping or waking. Natural dreams can range from those being full of love and peace to nightmares and are often the product of what we have been thinking about or desiring in previous days.

Isaiah 29:8 speaks of these types of dreams:

> . . .as when a hungry man dreams that he is eating, but he awakens, and his hunger remains; as when a thirsty man dreams he is drinking; but he awakens faint, with his thirst unquenched. (NIV)

Notice that the prophet does not say that such dreams are supernatural revelations from God.

I have known Christians who claimed that God gave them supernatural dreams, even though these "revelations" spoke contrary to the teachings of the Holy Scriptures. I know one person who has had dreams from God, but has also had natural dreams in which a relative spoke things contrary to the teachings of Scripture. This person did not test these latter dreams by Scripture and wrongly assumed they were God-given. Any dream that contradicts

Scripture is not from God.

Nightmares can result from overeating prior to going to bed, from watching a horror movie, or from allowing oneself to be ruled by fear. According to Ecclesiastes 5:3, natural dreams can result from cares:

As a dream comes when there are many cares. . . . (NIV)

A Warning

Be wary of preachers and lay people who suggest that we should record most or all of our dreams, expecting that each one contains messages from God. I read a Christian book recently that made such a suggestion. The same book also urged that we should ask God for interpretations for all of our dreams.

Such recommendations, if followed, will result in many Christians thinking that their merely natural dreams are God-given supernatural phenomena. Much deception will result for those who follow such advice.

Occultic Dream Guides

Christians who gullibly accept the writings and advice of all professional psychologists are in great danger. More and more professional psychologists are mixing occult-psychic ideas with their psychological theories. For example, some psychologists teach that all or most natural dreams can be interpreted according to occultic dream interpretation guides.

For Simplicity's Sake

Since the terms *dreams* and *visions* are used in so many different ways by Christians, it is little wonder there is much confusion. For simplicity's sake, it may be far more sensible to use the word *dream* in Christian circles to refer only to two different things; supernatural dreams and natural dreams, both of which occur only when one is asleep or partially asleep. It may be far better to find some other word or expression to describe the other two usages of the word.

8
How To Test
Dreams and Visions

Many may wonder, "How can I know the difference between a dream or vision from God and those of human or satanic origin?"

We can test the source of a dream or vision in three main ways. (The tests below are given mainly to help us distinguish God-given supernatural dreams and visions from those from other sources. But it can be used also to distinguish the godly-use-of-human imagination-meditation visions from those of fleshly and satanic origins and to distinguish godly-use-of-human imagination-meditation dreams from those of fleshly and natural origins.)

The First Test:
Agreement With Scripture

The main means by which we can distinguish dreams and visions of God from those of mere human origin or satanic origin (in the case of visions) is by checking to see if everything that occurs and is spoken in the dream or vision is in *total agreement with the teachings of the Scriptures taken as a whole* (see 2 Timothy 3:16-17; Acts 17:10-11; 1 Corinthians 14:37-38; Mark 7:1-13; Joshua 1:8;

John 10:35; Romans 15:4; Acts 24:14; 1 Corinthians 4:6; 2 Peter 1:20-21).

If anything that occurs or is spoken in the dream or vision is even slightly contrary to the teachings of Scripture, it is either from human origin or is satanic.

Even if a spiritual being appears in a vision and talks of Jesus, God the Father, and the Holy Spirit and quotes a few verses of Scripture, but interprets these verses inconsistently to the clear interpretations of other verses, this being is a demon in disguise. Matthew 4:5-6 reveals that Satan can mention God and even quote verses of Scripture in order to deceive. Jesus' response to Satan in Matthew 4:7 reveals that the enemy quotes verses of Scripture out of context and contrary to the meanings of other verses.

In Galatians 1:8, the Apostle Paul warned us of spiritual beings appearing to us in visions and preaching a gospel that is different from the one he taught: *"But even if we or an angel from heaven should preach a gospel other than the one we preached to you, let him be eternally condemned!"* (NIV).

Paul declared that such beings should be eternally condemned.

Specific Scriptural Principles

No dream or vision is from God unless it is in agreement with the objective principles of the Holy Scriptures:

● *"So whether you eat or drink or whatever you do, do it all for the glory of God"* (1 Corinthians 10:31, NIV).

A dream or a vision is not from God if it leads us to do anything which does not bring glory to God in some way. Doing *all* for the glory of God means that we think, speak and perform every deed in such a way that it encourages others or ourselves to honor and value God above everyone and everything else.

- *"But seek ye first the kingdom of God, and his righteousness; and all these things shall be added unto you"* (Matthew 6:33, AV).

The kingdom of God relates to God's rule in heaven and the spiritual world (see 2 Timothy 4:18), but it also involves His rule over our human spirit, mind and body (see Luke 17:20-21) and over the daily activities of our lives (see Matthew 7:21).

A dream or vision is not from God unless it guides us into allowing Him to rule over some part of our daily thoughts, feelings and actions. If it encourages us to be self-reliant, self-centered or proud, or if it encourages others to focus more attention and love on us or some other person or thing than on the Lord Jesus, that dream or vision is not from God.

- The Scriptures command us to help our Christian brothers and sisters in both spiritual and natural matters (see Hebrews 10:24, Philippians 2:4). They also admonish us to assist our non-Christian family members or associates to turn to the Lord Jesus (see Matthew 28:19-20). A dream or vision cannot be from God if it leads us to do something contrary to this.

Other important scriptural principles could be added to the above list.

Pastoral Assistance

If one is uncertain whether or not a vision or dream is in agreement with the Scriptures, he should ask the advice of his local church leaders. Seek the counsel of born-again church leaders who are centered in Scripture and not bound by man-made religious traditions. Otherwise, the counsel may be ungodly.

Choose a leader whose life expresses the fruit of the Holy Spirit, such as love, patience, kindness, unselfishness and humility (see Galatians 5:22). Look for someone whose ambition is to be fully dependent upon God and His Holy Spirit and who is full of love and devotion for Jesus. Prayerfully consider the advice of such a leader, while carefully examining the verses of Scripture he shares.

The Second Test:
An Inner Witness

If a dream or vision passes the first test—in agreement with the teachings of the Holy Scriptures—then we need to apply the second test. The next step involves discerning whether God the Holy Spirit affirms to our spirit that the dream or vision is from Him. This inner witness of the Holy Spirit is spoken of in Romans 8:16, Colossians 3:15, and Philippians 4:7.

The inner witness involves the Holy Spirit giving us a *peace* or *joy*, or both, in our spirit when we have some revelation from God in our mind.

The inner witness can come also in the form of an *uneasy, tight feeling in our spirit* when we have something in our mind that is not God's will. These sensations of peace and joy, or uneasiness and tightness *are not emotional feelings.* Instead they are spiritual perceptions occurring in our spirit.

The following is an example of the difference between emotional feelings and the inner witness of the Holy Spirit: A Christian man can feel the emotion of joy when thinking about marrying a particular Christian woman. At the same time he may have an inner witness of uneasiness or tightness from the Holy Spirit in his spirit revealing that it is not God's will for him to marry her.

(For more details about the inner witness of the Holy Spirit, refer to my book, *How To Recognize God's Voice.* The more we follow the practices spoken of in Chapter 16, "Improving Your Ability To Recognize God's Voice," the easier it will be for us to recognize the inner witness of the Holy Spirit.)

If a person has a vision, he needs to ask himself whether or not he sensed peace or joy in his spirit while he was having it. In the weeks following the vision, as he waits on God in prayer, does he continue to sense the peace or joy in his spirit that the vision is from God? One needs to be still before God for more than a few minutes regarding such matters.

If the sense of peace and joy are absent in one's spirit regarding the source of a vision, but instead an uneasy tightness persists, one must conclude that the vision was from demons or a product of human imagination.

Since we are asleep when we dream, it is sometimes difficult for us to remember whether we had a sense of peace or joy in our spirit at the time. Therefore, dreams are best tested later by checking to see if we have a sense of peace or joy in our spirit as we wait on God in prayer asking Him to reveal if this dream was from Him.

My saying that a dream or vision from God will be accompanied by the peace of the Holy Spirit, does not mean that the receiver will never be troubled by the revelation in the dream or vision once it has ceased.

For example, Daniel 7:28 shows that after Daniel had received a vision from God, he was greatly troubled in thought and his face turned pale. This God-given vision had revealed to Daniel the terrible persecutions that a wicked king would inflict on God's people (see 7:23-25).

The Third Test: Fulfillment

Not all dreams and visions involve predictions of the future. If, however, a dream or vision does contain a prediction, we must test it by the principles found in Deuteronomy 18:21-22:

> You may say to yourselves, "How can we know when a message has not been spoken by the Lord?" If what a prophet proclaims in the name of the Lord does not take place or come true, that is a message the Lord has not spoken. The prophet has spoken presumptuously. . . . (NIV)

These verses relate to the testing of the predictions of prophets. But since God speaks often to prophets in supernatural dreams and visions (see Numbers 12:6), these verses can also relate to the testing of predictive dreams and visions.

The prophet Moses' words in Deuteronomy 18:21-22 reveal one of the many reasons why we should regard with suspicion the so-called "visions of Mary" at Fatima in Portugal. Note that the New Catholic Encyclopedia states that "saint" Lucia—one of the children who saw a spiritual entity professing to be Mary—prophesied wrongly on October 13, 1917, that World War I would end that day or very soon afterwards.[2] World War I ended instead one year and one month later. Similarly, Lucia claimed that this same spiritual entity told her in 1917, "You saw Hell where the souls of poor sinners go. In order to save them God wishes to establish in the world devotion to my Immaculate Heart. If people do what I ask, many souls will be saved and there will be peace. The war is going to end. But if people do not stop offending God, another, even worse, will *begin in the reign of Pius XI.*"[3] This was

---

[2] *New Catholic Encyclopedia*, Volume 5, (McGraw Hill Book Co., New York, 1967) page 856.
[3] Ibid.

another false prophecy because World War II began in September 1939. Pope Pius XI was dead at the time.

Fulfillment Alone Is Not Sufficient

To test a dream or vision only by the third test is not sufficient. The predictions of a dream or vision can come to pass, but it still not be from God.

For example, I may have a dream in which I see myself stealing an expensive watch from a shop. I may then tell a friend about the dream. A demon may hear what I said. At a later time when I am shopping, the demon may tempt me to steal an expensive watch. If I were to yield to this temptation, I might say to myself: "See! What God predicted that He wanted me to do came to pass."

The above dream would not be from God, because it suggested that I disobey one of His commands recorded in the Scriptures. Ephesians 4:28 states:

He who has been stealing must steal no longer. . . . (NIV)

Therefore, even though this dream passed the third test, it did not pass the first one.

All dreams and visions that contain a prediction of the future, must also be tried by the first test: Are they contrary to the teachings of Scripture?

Deuteronomy 13:1-4 confirms that the fulfillment of a dream's prediction does not necessarily mean that it was God-given:

If a prophet, or one who foretells by dreams, appears among you and announces to you a miraculous sign or wonder, and if the sign or wonder of which he has spoken takes place, and he says, "Let us follow other gods" (gods you have not known) "and let us worship them," you must not listen to the words of that prophet or dreamer. The Lord your God is testing you to find out whether you love him with all your heart and with all your soul. It is the Lord your God you must follow, and him you must revere. Keep his commands and obey him; serve him and hold fast to him. (NIV)

These verses indicate that God's commands have greater authority than fulfilled dreams. All dreams, visions and miraculous signs must be tested by God's written commands found in His Scriptures.

A Personal Example

Six years before I was married, I had a dream in which I saw a young woman with whom I was working at the time. In the dream, I was not far from the woman when I felt myself being pulled away from her. I felt any possible interest in her being changed to feelings of mere friendship.

I had never established any type of relationship with this person. But I had been praying for a few weeks before then asking if the Lord willed me later to marry her. (In the years that followed, I prayed the same prayer about all the Christian young women with whom I was friendly.)

The first test we must apply to this dream is whether it told me to do anything contrary to the Holy Scriptures. The dream passed this test.

Another aspect of this same test asked the question, "Does the dream encourage me not to put God first?" The answer in this case was, "No." Therefore, the dream passed this test.

Similarly, we must ask: Did the dream encourage me to not seek God's kingdom first in the matter? The answer again is, "No." So, the dream passed this test also.

The second test we must apply is whether I had a sense of peace or joy, or both, in my spirit in the days or weeks following as I waited on God in prayer, asking if it was from Him or from my natural mind. I found that as I committed this dream to Him in prayer, He gave me a peace in my spirit that this dream was indeed from Him.

Since this dream did not contain a prediction of the future, I did not need to apply the principles of the third test.

Therefore, I obeyed the guidance given in this God-given dream.

None of Us Are Infallible

Even though I have had a number of God-given dreams and visions, it would be wrong if I left my readers with the impression that I am some sort of infallible tester of dreams and visions. We can all make mistakes in our analysis of such things. But if we do make a mistake, we should confess our error to God and trust Him to help us be less easily deceived in the future.

9
Johanna Michaelsen

An example of our need to check thoroughly the source of any vision that we may have, can be seen in the life of Johanna Michaelsen[1]. Although she prayed to the Lord, Johanna also practiced E.S.P. and other psychic powers.

At one time, Johanna, along with some other psychics, practiced spiritualistic techniques with the aim of having visions of their so-called "spirit counsellors". On the basis of Revelation 3:20, where Jesus Christ said, ". . .*I stand at the door and knock. If anyone hears my voice and opens the door, I will go in and eat with him, and he with me"* (NIV), Johanna asked Jesus to be her "spirit guide" and appear to her regularly in vision form. She interpreted Revelation 3:20 contrary to many other verses of Scripture which speak of the need to accept Jesus Christ as our one and only Lord and God, not just as one of the so-called "higher spirit guides".

After she had done the above, a spirit-being claiming to be Jesus Christ appeared to her regularly in visions. The being spoke to Johanna in a gentle voice and with a loving, shining face.

At one time, the creature appeared with a translucent glow and held what seemed to be "a flame of purification" in his hand. He poured the flames into Johanna's hands.

---

[1]Johanna Michaelsen, *The Beautiful Side of Evil*. (Harvest House Publishers, Eugene, Oregon, United States, 1982).

As a result, her hands felt a burning sensation and yet were cold.

Note that just prior to this experience, Johanna had been praying, "Almighty God, more than anything else, You know I love You and want to serve You. Help me now become an instrument of Your hands. I give myself to You, O Lord. Guide us now in this work. . .*Protect us from any evil being* who would hinder this work which You have set before me. Let Your perfect will be done, Holy God."

Warned by God

Considering the fact that Johanna Michaelsen prayed these noble words and specifically asked for God's protection from demons, one might be surprised to know what she later learned about the being who appeared to her claiming to be Jesus. Johanna had been *warned many times* previously by God through her committed Christian sister and by a Christian named Kim that her psychic and spiritualism practices were demonic.

Even though she continued to pray and say good things to God, Johanna chose to ignore these warnings. She had entertained some doubts about these practices, but she chose to suppress the questions, assuring herself that these "spirit counsellors" could not be satanic. After all, hadn't they been helping her psychic friends perform miraculous healings? Johanna imagined foolishly that Satan and his demons cannot also do wonders.

Satanic Healings

According to God's Word, Satan and demons can cause people to be sick (see Job 2:7; Luke 13:11-16; and Acts

10:38). Johanna failed to realize that in order to bring about a healing, all Satan and his demons have to do is remove their sickness-causing power from the afflicted person.

Job 2:7 says:

> So Satan went out from the presence of the Lord and afflicted Job with painful sores from the soles of his feet to the top of his head. (NIV)

Luke 13:10-11 and 15-16 says:

> On a Sabbath Jesus was teaching in one of the synagogues, and a woman was there who had been **crippled by a spirit** for eighteen years. She was bent over and could not straighten up at all. . . The Lord answered him, "You hypocrites! Doesn't each of you on the Sabbath untie his ox or donkey from the stall and lead it out to give it water? Then should not this woman, a daughter of Abraham, whom **Satan has kept bound** for eighteen long years, be set free on the Sabbath day from what bound her? (N.I.V., bold type added)

Acts 10:38 says:

> . . .God anointed Jesus of Nazareth with the Holy Spirit and power, and. . .he went around doing good and **healing all who were under the power of the devil**, because God was with him. (N.I.V., bold type added)

Only God knows whether or not Satan and his demons have the power to bring about healings even when they have not originally caused the sickness. But whatever the case, they have deceived thousands of people in non-Christian religions and in occult-psychic groups by performing healings and other miracles for them.

Such simulated miracles must be clearly distinguished from genuine healings from God which occur among born-again believers in the wonderful Name of the Lord Jesus

Christ. The Holy Scriptures are full of accounts of such happenings.

Remember also that not all sickness is caused by Satan and his demons. Some sickness is the result of contact with harmful insecticides and asbestos, exposure to nuclear radiation and such.

Infiltration of Occult

Some non-Evangelical, non-Pentecostal, non-Charismatic church groups are presently involved in forms of occultic healing. These "healers" are not born-again, yet they lay hands on the sick claiming that God flows through them. Many of these teach pagan Eastern religion meditation as well as yoga techniques. We must warn people of the difference between these and godly, born-again ministries of healing.

Occult-witchcraft spiritual healers are a growing breed also. Some of these teach the view held by some pagan Eastern religions that God lives in every person, or the spirit of every person is a god. They claim proudly that they can heal people.

Spiritualist "churches" also are practitioners in demonic healings. These people have church services, but also contact demons who masquerade as good spirit guides or dead humans. This latter practice is called mediums or channeling.

Which Jesus?

After the above events, Johanna visited her Christian sister, who challenged Johanna with questions such as, "How do you know the Jesus you see in your laboratory is the Jesus of the Bible?" "Even though one of your psychic friends performs psychic healings, how can you be sure that it is God and not demons who is responsible?" Johanna admitted to herself that she could not be sure.

"Good" Spirits Reveal Their True Character

Sometime later, Johanna decided to accept Jesus Christ of Nazareth as the Sacred Scriptures reveal Him to be, *not as she wanted Him to be.* As she traveled to the home of some committed Christians, where she was going to accept Jesus Christ as her only Lord and God, the spirits who previously had claimed to be Jesus and other good beings, turned on her with violent rage. The creatures shrieked in hideous laughter that they were going to kill her. Then they tried to choke the life from her.

As soon as Johanna arrived at the home of her Christian friends, one of them took authority over the spirits in the Name of the Lord Jesus Christ. The beings had no choice but to cease their evil. Johanna then accepted the Jesus Christ of the Bible as her Lord and Saviour.

Even so, the "spirit counsellors" still tried to deceive her. Once a spirit claiming to be Jesus appeared to her in vision form. When Johanna confronted it in the Name of Jesus Christ of Nazareth, this so-called "Jesus" smashed several physical objects and then vanished.

A Solemn Warning

This true story reveals how Christians must be very careful before accepting any vision of a being claiming to be Jesus, the angel Gabriel, the angel Michael, Mary, Joseph, or any other spiritual being, as being God-given and not satanic.

Johanna Michaelsen's story is one reason why I have grave doubts about the source of the so-called visions of Mary at Fatima, La Salette, Lourdes, Medjugorgje in Yugoslavia, and other places, and the healings associated with them. This is especially true since some of the utterances spoken at these places by the being claiming to be Mary, contradict the teachings of the Lord Jesus Christ, and the Apostles and Prophets as recorded in the Sacred Scriptures.

Joseph Smith, founder of the Mormon cult, and Mohammed, founder of Islam, both claimed to have had God-given visions of great angels of God. However, these angels who appeared to Joseph Smith and Mohammed disagreed with the teachings of Jesus and His Apostles and Prophets regarding many things. This is a clear indication of the source of these spirits masquerading as great angels of God.

According to Acts 16:16-18, a religious person may speak many of God's truths, yet still be possessed by an evil spirit:

> *Once when we were going to the place of prayer, we were met by a slave girl who had a spirit by which she predicted the future. She earned a great deal of money for her owners by fortune-telling. This girl followed Paul and the rest of us, shouting, "These men are servants of the Most High God, who are telling you the way to be saved." She kept this up for many days. Finally Paul became so troubled that he turned around and said to the spirit, "In the name of Jesus Christ I command you to come out of her!" At that moment the spirit left her. (NIV)*

Note that the words this girl spoke by the demon were great Christian truths. Demons will even speak part of the gospel and some Christian truths, if this enables them to gain some influence over their churchgoing prey. Many churchgoers think that Satan and demons do nothing but lie. This is wrong. Evil spirits often lie, but they will also speak truth if it improves their attempts to control their listeners.

10
Other People's Dreams and Visions For Us

We must be aware of the danger of accepting without question a dream or vision some other person claims God has revealed to him for us.

All Christians, including the most godly preachers, can make mistakes in getting guidance from God. Some preachers who have been used greatly by God in different ways, have given to others so-called "visions from God" that were merely the product of their own fleshly imaginations. Others have maintained that their own fleshly dreams (occurring while awake) and natural dreams (occurring while asleep) are God-inspired revelations.

Some recipients of these so-called "divine interventions" have accepted these gullibly without examining them according to the standards provided in Chapter 8, "How To Test Dreams and Visions". As a result, many individuals have been led out of God's will in various matters.

Some Christians have not only been gullible about the so-called "divine visions and dreams" of some church leaders, they have also failed to test the "divine revelations" of lay relatives and friends. For example, some have been led into marriages that were not God's will by not testing the "divine dreams and visions" of others for them.

A Gullible Prophet

The danger of accepting an untested "revelation" from another person is seen in 1 Kings 13:1-32.

These verses record how a prophet of God from Judah had been told by God to go to the city of Bethel in the Northern Kingdom of Israel. God gave the prophet some prophecies against the pagan altar that King Jeroboam had set up there. God also told him to foretell the birth of a godly king called Josiah. (Compare 1 Kings 13:2 to 2 Kings 22:1— 23:30.) The Lord commanded the prophet to eat no bread and drink no water in Bethel.

An old, partially backslidden prophet who lived in Bethel heard what had happened, followed after the man of God from Judah and found him under an oak tree. The old prophet invited him home to eat bread. At first, the prophet from Judah refused, quoting what God had commanded him. Then the old prophet said:

> I too am a prophet, as you are. And an angel said to me by the word of the Lord: "Bring him back with you to your house so that he may eat bread and drink water" .... (1 Kings 13:18, NIV)

The prophet from Judah was impressed by this so-called "word of the Lord". He went home with the old prophet and ate in his house. The prophet from Judah did not realize that the old seer had *lied* to him. Tragically, the prophet from Judah lost his life as a result. We must test carefully the "revelations" others wish to give us.

Confirmation of "Revelations"

Acts 20:22-23 and Acts 21:10-13, taken together, give the correct procedure of dealing with "revelations", or "words from the Lord" that others wish to give us about matters on which the Scriptures do not reveal God's specific will. Acts 20:22-23 records the words of the Apostle Paul:

> And now, **compelled by the Spirit**, I am going to Jerusalem, not knowing what will happen to me there. I only know that in every city the Holy Spirit warns me that prison and hardships are facing me. (NIV, bold type added)

Acts 21:10-13 records:

> After we had been there a number of days, a prophet named Agabus came down from Judea. Coming over to us, he took Paul's belt, tied his own hands and feet with it and said, "The Holy Spirit says, 'In this way the Jews of Jerusalem will bind the owner of this belt and will hand him over to the Gentiles.'" When we heard this, we and the people there pleaded with Paul not to go up to Jerusalem. Then Paul answered, "Why are you weeping and breaking my heart? I am ready not only to be bound, but also to die in Jerusalem for the name of the Lord Jesus." (NIV)

Agabus was a highly respected New Testament prophet who had been used previously by the Lord to warn the early Church of a coming famine (see Acts 11:27-29). Do not, however, be fooled into thinking that Paul accepted everything Agabus prophesied, just because Agabus was a respected prophet, and because he had earlier success in predicting coming disaster.

Paul accepted Agabus' revelation as God-given only because God the Holy Spirit earlier had revealed to Paul similar concerns. What Agabus prophesied largely *confirmed* what the Holy Spirit already had told Paul.

11
Dangerous Trends

When I was writing my book, *How To Recognize God's Voice*, in the early 1980s, I warned against our setting human reason on a pinnacle above the guidance of the Holy Spirit. At the time, I saw much evidence of this *overly rationalistic* type of Christianity, which exalts human reason to a position above that given by the Sacred Scriptures.

Some Christians argued that God gave them their ability to reason in order to equip them to make wise choices— who to marry, where to live, what job to have, and so on. They tended also not to accept any of God's miraculous workings, unless they could be explained logically.

Segments of the church worldwide are still caught in this overly rational brand of Christianity.

In recent years, however, a new form of extremism has emerged. This new trend is an *overly mystical* approach to Christianity which gives human imagination or the ability to fantasize a place of extreme prominence. Such an over-emphasis is contrary to Scripture taken as a whole.

Many have been attracted to this extremely mystical approach to Christianity out of a desire to know God more deeply. But they are unaware of the dangers of this approach.

To claim that Jesus was not from the Western culture, but was an Easterner, to support this ultra-mystical view of Christianity, is a subtle deception. Jesus' words support neither the Western brand of over-rationalism, nor the Eastern type of ultra-mysticism. Jesus never quoted from any of the Greek rationalist philosophers or the Eastern mystics.

We see in the Scriptures that God is the author of reason and imagination. Both of these abilities play important roles in our lives. But an overemphasis on the importance of either, to the detriment of our reliance on biblical guidance or on the leading of the Holy Spirit, will provoke great difficulties for ourselves and for the local church.

12
Good Teaching, But. . .!

In recent years, some books have been published that emphasized the godly-use-of-human imagination-meditation type of visions.

The better of these books focus correctly on the fact that the use of the human imagination is wrong if it results in our imagining or mentally picturing things that are contrary to the teachings of the Sacred Scriptures taken as a whole. These authors should be commended for this.

The better of these volumes also have taught some splendid concepts regarding the importance of our deeply loving and knowing the Lord Jesus, repentance and confession of sins, having godly motives, spending much time in prayer, fasting sometimes, and of praising God. The finer of these also have emphasized correctly that some supernatural visions may not be spectacular, but are merely visual impressions placed by God in our minds.

We must, however, question their teaching that the more we use our imagination to visualize Scriptural references or to fantasize encounters with the Lord Jesus (e.g. imagining talking to Him face to face), the more God will give us supernatural visions.

Akin to this is the highly questionable teaching that the more we look for God-given visions and dreams, the more He will give such revelations.

Shaky Biblical Foundations

One Christian author lists page after page of Scripture verses referring to dreams or visions. He does this as supposed evidence that God will give us dreams and visions more frequently, if we keep looking into the spiritual world.

This, however, is a faulty conclusion. Quoting extensive lists of Scripture passages regarding the frequency of angelic visitations does not prove that continually looking for angels will improve one's prospects of seeing them more frequently.

Twisting Verses In Daniel

This same author uses verses such as Daniel 7:1, 9 and 13 as supposed biblical confirmation that God wants us to actively seek to have God-given dreams and visions regularly.

In their original context, the verses found in Daniel do not infer that God granted the visions and dreams mentioned here because Daniel was looking for and seeking after them. Instead, Daniel 7:1-28 reveals that Daniel was lying on his bed when *God chose* to give him a dream and some visions. Then Daniel merely looked at what God chose to show him supernaturally. Daniel was *not looking for* God-given dreams and visions. Instead, he *looked at* what God chose to reveal to him.

Daniel's "looking," mentioned in verses 9 and 13, was *in response to* what God already began to show him in verse 1. Daniel *focused on God*, not on a specific method of guidance, such as God-given dreams and visions. Because he had his focus in the right place, he was receptive to however God chose to speak to him.

Daniel was willing to receive guidance from God in the form of God-given dreams and visions. His response to his dream and visions proves this. But note that prior to receiving guidance, Daniel *did not specify to God* what supernatural means he preferred God to use.

Evidence of this is seen in other segments of the Book of Daniel. For instance, in chapter 2, verses 17-18, Daniel encouraged his friends to seek God's guidance. He did not tell them, however, to ask God specifically for a dream or a vision. Nevertheless, in His sovereign will, God chose to speak to Daniel in this instance by a vision (see Daniel 2:19).

Several Scripture passages disclose that God is always ready to speak to us from His written Word as we read it or hear it preached (see 2 Timothy 3:15-17; Joshua 1:8; Romans 10:15-17; Romans 15:4; Luke 24:27; 1 Corinthians 14:37-38; and 2 Peter 1:20-21).

The Bible contains no promises giving us the right to specify by what method God may speak to us. It does provide a general promise that the Holy Spirit will guide us (see John 16:13). But it is up to God the Father to decide *when* and *how* He will speak to us by His Spirit.

We have the God-given right to seek His guidance, certain that He will answer (see James 1:5-8). Whether it is by an inner witness (see Romans 8:16), a still small voice (see 1 Kings 19:12), a dream, a vision, an angel or by some other means, *it is up to Him to decide.*

It is dangerous to look for angels to appear regularly and try to pressure God to speak to us with an audible voice. It is also dangerous to do the same with God-given dreams and visions.

Twisting Other Verses

Some have suggested recently that because the Apostle John said, "I looked" (see Revelation 4:1), and some of the Old Testament Prophets said that they "looked",[1] they were seeking God-given visions and dreams constantly.

A close examination of these verses reveals that they do not refer to the Apostle John and the Prophets following some sort of technique or formula of how to look for, seek after, and obtain God-given dreams and visions.

This becomes clear when we read Revelation 1:10-19, which introduces the events found in Revelation 4:1. In Revelation 1:10-12, God told John to record what He would show him. The other verses listed in the footnote also refer to the Prophets looking at what *God had decided* to show them.

Other verses, such as Psalms 25:15, 123:1, 141:8, Isaiah 8:17 and 17:7, are quoted also as supposed support of this false teaching. When we look at these verses, though, we find that they have *nothing to do with our looking for God-given dreams or visions*, but rather refer to seeking after or looking for God Himself, His presence and a stronger relationship to Him.

James 4:2 also has been quoted to suggest that God will not give us dreams and visions unless we ask for them. Such usage of this passage involves interpreting it contrary to many other biblical verses which speak of God giving dreams and visions to people who did not request them.

Verses such as Psalm 119:18, Isaiah 44:18, Jeremiah 5:21, Matthew 13:15-16, John 12:40, Acts 28:27, and Romans 11:8 are quoted by one author as supposed biblical proof for his teaching that we need to seek God diligently, asking

---

[1] See Genesis 18:1-2; 31:10-12; Exodus 3:1-2; 16:9-10; Joshua 5:13; 1 Chronicles 21:16; Daniel 10:5-16; 12:15; Ezekiel 1:1-4; 2:9; 8:3-7; 44:1-5; Zechariah 1:18; 2:1; 4:2; 5:5; 6:1.

Him to open the eyes and ears of our hearts so we can have God-given visions often. When we examine these verses, however, we find that they speak of *spiritual revelations* from God *in general*, not specifically of God-given visions and dreams.

These verses cover revelations by God-given dreams and visions, but they refer equally to the other means of revelation the Holy Spirit may use to speak to us. These other methods include the inner witness of the Holy Spirit, the inner voice of the Holy Spirit, signs in our circumstances, God's audible voice, angelic visitations, and so on. (Refer to my book *How To Recognize God's Voice* for more details of these.)

It is wrong to use the verses listed above in an attempt to prove doctrines which over-emphasize the place of dreams and visions in our receiving of guidance from the Holy Spirit. Such an over-emphasis results in a de-emphasizing of other means that the Holy Spirit may prefer to use to speak to us.

Although passages such as Psalm 119:18, Isaiah 44:18, Jeremiah 5:21 and Acts 28:27 cover revelations by God-given dreams and visions, these verses do not authorize us to dictate to Him by which means His Holy Spirit may speak to us. God may wish to give one person a number of supernatural dreams and visions. He may prefer to use dissimilar means to give others similar revelations.

Acts 2:17

Some claim that Acts 2:17 reveals that God expects all or most Christians to be looking for and seeking to have God-given dreams and visions almost daily or weekly. Such a suggestion is nonsense.

An examination of this verse, reveals that it makes no

mention of Christians' looking for or seeking after God-given dreams and visions. The passage merely says:

> . . .and your young men shall see visions, and your old men shall dream dreams. (Authorized Version)

It is dangerous to look for "hidden," extra meanings to any passage of Scripture, Acts 2:17 included.

Observe also that one can fall into error by attempting to interpret Acts 2:17 ultra-specifically. If this verse is given an overly specific interpretation, it would mean that God gives only young men supernatural visions and only old men supernatural dreams.

Such an overly specific interpretation, however, does not agree with facts surrounding the Book of Revelation, which was written by the Apostle John in about 96 A.D.[2] Banished to the island of Patmos, the Apostle received awesome God-given visions (see Revelation 1:9-20). The Lord Jesus had died and resurrected when the Apostle John had been a young man. Now about 66 years later, as an old man in his 80s or 90s, he saw the visions recorded in the last book of the Bible. These facts do not agree with an overly specific interpretation of Acts 2:17 which would suggest that old men are given dreams by God and not visions. Even if the Book of Revelation was written earlier in about A.D. 70 as some suggest, John would still have not been a young man. He would have been in his 50s or 60s..

Acts 2:17 is merely saying that in the last days God will give supernatural dreams and visions to His people. It is a *general* promise of God to His church as a whole. If we wish to use the verse to prove that God wants each of us to seek to have supernatural dreams and visions every

---

[2]John D. Davis, *Davis Dictionary of the Bible* (Baker Book House, Grand Rapids, Michigan), page 689.

five minutes, we must add a "hidden," extra meaning to the verse.

Reasons For Errors

One of the main reasons for these kinds of errors about visions and dreams is that many Christians do not know how to distinguish God-given manifestations from godly-use-of-human imagination-meditation types of visions and dreams.

Another basis of error is that many Christians cannot distinguish between God-given visions and dreams and fleshly visions and dreams.

A third reason for error is that some Christians do not know the differences between God-given dreams and natural dreams.

These various types of visions and dreams are mixed together so often in some teaching, it is little wonder many Christians are confused.

A Qualifying Remark

In Chapter 3, "Godly Use of Imagination-Meditation Visions," I spoke of the godly use of human imagination in meditating on things recorded in the Sacred Scriptures. God may decide to grant us a supernatural vision while we are using our imaginations in this godly way. But to infer that the more we employ our imagination to meditate on Him and His Word, the more He will give us more supernatural visions, is to suggest that we can manipulate Him.

13
Seers

In the Old Testament, God's prophets were often called "seers" (see 1 Chronicles 29:29; 2 Chronicles 9:29; 19:2; 1 Samuel 9:9). On this basis, some have tried recently to prove that the prophets practiced techniques of specifically looking for and seeking after God-given dreams and visions constantly.

The correct definition of the word, *seer*, however, differs greatly from this understanding. In the Old Testament, a seer was a person whom *God chose* to receive various revelations of His will. These revelations were then to be declared often to others. Verses such as Jeremiah 1:5, 20:9, 1 Corinthians 12:28-29 and Ephesians 4:11 communicate the fact that God chooses whom He wishes to be His seers. These verses refute the idea that we can all become God's seers by learning various techniques which supposedly help us to see God-given visions and dreams more often.

> *And in the church* **God has appointed** *first of all apostles, second prophets, third teachers. . .Are all apostles? Are all prophets? Are all teachers?. . . . (1 Corinthians 12:28-29, NIV, bold type added)*

> *It was* **he who gave** *some to be apostles, some to be prophets, some to be evangelists. . . . (Ephesians 4:11, NIV, bold type added)*

These verses reveal that *some, not all* Christians are appointed by God as prophets.

God appointed Jeremiah as a prophet or seer *before* he had even heard of God, let alone learned any supposed techniques of trying to look for and seek after God-given dreams and visions:

> *Before I formed you in the womb I knew you, before you were born I set you apart;* **I appointed** *you as a prophet to the nations. (Jeremiah 1:5, NIV, bold type added)*

Any person who tries to become a prophet or seer by learning procedures and formulas for obtaining God-given revelations, is a *self-appointed* prophet or seer. In Matthew 7:15, Jesus warns us of false, self-commissioned prophets:

> *Watch out for false prophets. . . . (NIV)*

Other passages, such as 1 John 4:1 and 2 Peter 2:1, also speak of false prophets. Note, too, that God's seers did not just receive visions and dreams. He also gave His message to them by the still small voice (see 1 Kings 19:12), signs in circumstances (see Jeremiah 32:6-8; Isaiah 37:30-32), and by other means.

Self-appointed prophets are just as dangerous as self-appointed apostles, of whom the Apostle Paul warned us in 2 Corinthians 11:13.

"Learning" To Be A Prophet

Recent teachings claim that "the school of the prophets" that Samuel conducted was mainly for the purpose of instructing others in techniques of how to look for and have God-given visions and dreams (see 1 Samuel 19:20).

This interpretation is a total misrepresentation. Samuel conducted "the school of the prophets" to teach those whom God had selected to be prophets the principles of how to have a close personal relationship with Him, and similar Scriptural instructions.

It has been claimed recently that the reason why multitudes of people are not seers and prophets today is because no one is teaching them to be "lookers". Such beliefs *appeal to the pride* and *fleshly nature* of many Christians who would love to be a prophet, even though God has not called them to be one. It also sadly appeals to some devoted Christians who are looking for the means to know God better.

Those who are called by God to be prophets *can* resist His working in their hearts by choosing to disobey guidance He has revealed previously to them. The prophets Jonah (see Jonah 1:1-17) and Balaam (see Numbers 22:1-34; 2 Peter 2:15-16; Revelation 2:14; Numbers 25:1-3; 31:16) are two prime examples of this.

It is also true that one who is called to the ministry gift of a prophet can miss the calling by lack of awareness that God could use him in such a way.

This is different, however, from suggesting that a Christian will not see God-given dreams and visions in the future unless he is seeking them constantly.

Many Warnings

In Micah 3:5-7, God warned the people of seers who were not appointed by Him. That warning still applies today.

Many warnings are recorded in the Holy Scriptures about self-appointed seers and prophets having visions that were not from God. Ezekiel 13:4, 6-7 underscores the warnings:

> *Your prophets, O Israel, are like jackals among ruins. . .
> Their visions are* **false** *and their divinations a lie. They say,
> "The Lord declares," when* **the Lord has not sent them***;
> yet they expect their words to be fulfilled. Have you not seen*
> **false visions** *and uttered lying divinations when you say,
> "The Lord declares,"* **though I have not spoken***? (NIV,
> bold type added)*

The prophet Jeremiah also records warnings:

> *Then the Lord said to me, "The prophets are prophesying
> lies in my name.* **I have not sent them or appointed
> them or spoken to them.** *They are prophesying to you*
> **false visions***, divinations, idolatries and the* **delusions
> of their own minds.***" (Jeremiah 14:14, NIV, bold type
> added)*

> *This is what the Lord Almighty says: "Do not listen to
> what the prophets are prophesying to you; they fill you with
> false hopes. They speak* **visions from their own minds***,
> not from the mouth of the Lord." (Jeremiah 23:16, NIV, bold
> type added)*

These self-appointed prophets had fooled themselves into
thinking that they were having God-given visions and
revelations. As Jeremiah 14:14 infers, however, unless God
decides to give a supernatural vision to a person, nothing
is going to force God to give him one.

Some may think that self-manufactured visions were only
an Old Testament problem. But Colossians 2:18 reveals
that even in New Testament churches, people can be
tempted by pride to think that their imaginings are God-
given visions.

Jeremiah 23:30-32 warns of people claiming that they
had God-given dreams when they did not:

> *"Therefore," declares the Lord, "I am against the prophets
> who steal from one another words supposedly from me. Yes,"
> declares the Lord, "I am against the prophets who wag their*

*own tongues and yet declare, 'The Lord declares.' Indeed, I am against those who prophesy **false dreams**," declares the Lord. "They tell them and lead my people astray with their reckless lies, yet **I did not send or appoint them**. . . ." (NIV, bold type added)*

These verses reveal that such people were self-appointed prophets. They were not designated by God to receive their so-called God-given dreams and revelations.

Jeremiah 23:11 reveals that many of these self-called prophets continued to attend the God-appointed gatherings at His temple in Jerusalem. They did not set up their own separate pagan religion. Because these false prophets were active in Temple ceremonies, they were used by Satan to corrupt even this God-ordained worship. Jeremiah 23:15 says:

. . . from the prophets of Jerusalem ungodliness has spread throughout the land. (NIV)[1]

Difference Between The Gift Of Prophecy And Being A Prophet

According to 1 Corinthians 14:1, any Christian on occasion may exercise the spiritual gift of prophecy. This gift is for strengthening, encouraging and comforting the local body of Christ (see 1 Corinthians 14:3-4).

Many, however, choose to ignore the fact that Ephesians 4:11 and 1 Corinthians 12:28-29 specify that only a certain number of people are called to the ministry gift of a prophet.

Similarly, even though every Christian on occasion can teach another person something from the Scriptures, only

---

[1]Refer to Chapter 8, *How To Test Dreams and Visions*, which gives details of how to test whether or not a dream or vision is from God.

a certain number of people are called to the ministry gift of a teacher. As John the Baptist said about ministry:

> . . . *A man can receive* **only what is given him from heaven.** *(John 3:27, NIV, bold type added)*

Unless a person is already a church leader, or feels God's call to become one in the future, he should not entertain the thought that he may have the ministry gift of a prophet. He may have exercised the simple gift of prophecy many times, but he does not have the ministry of a prophet. Originally, Amos was a shepherd and Elisha a farmer, but then they were called by God into ministry (see Amos 7:14-15 and 1 Kings 19:15-21). After beginning to function as prophets, Amos and Elisha were used by God to operate more than just the simple gift of prophecy.

Note also that a person can be functioning as a New Testament prophet before they are recognized as such by the Church.

First Corinthians 14, the main biblical section dealing with the simple gift of prophecy, does not say that this gift relates to predicting the future. Deuteronomy 18:21-22 and Acts 11:27-29 reveal that the ministry gift of a prophet sometimes involves God enabling the person to foretell forthcoming events.

Personal Experiences

I have seen much religious "flesh" manifested when certain lay people who are not called to the ministry, assume that their God-given dreams, visions and manifestations of the simple gift of prophecy, qualify them to be known as a New Testament prophet.

Such false claims often breed hurt, bitterness and

divisions. These self-appointed "prophets" unwittingly open themselves up to a demon who tries to control others and the local church through the "prophet". These self-appointed prophets lack godly humility, or they manifest a false humility. Some manifest humility as lay people, but later change when self-delusions about their "prophetic ministry" take over.

Much damage is done also when those who are called by God to the ministries of shepherd, teacher, evangelist or apostle, disobey Him by assuming the mantle of a prophet.

Once a self-appointed prophet gave me a sealed letter to pass on to a local pastor. The "prophet" did not tell me what was inside. Later the pastor told me that the letter contained threats of divine judgment if the pastor refused to bring himself under the "prophet's" control.

This was a sad case. The "prophet" previously had been a fine Christian. Then he fell into pride and became influenced by a demon which made him cry out terribly. Often in the middle of a sentence, he would moan loudly for a few seconds and then continue talking. He refused to submit to any pastor and began to attend church only on rare occasions. The man claimed to be God's main chosen instrument in one of the major cities in Australia.

Another recent tragic case in Sydney, Australia, involved a lay-person who claimed to be a prophet with miraculous powers. Step by step the woman came to exercise greater and greater authority and control over her followers. In the end, these people began to regard her as being divine. Finally, she threatened divine judgment on anyone who failed to follow her instructions. Many of her disciples believed these threats and obeyed her as if she were Jesus Christ.

A True Prophet Of God

A true prophet of God leads people to concentrate on *Jesus Christ* and *plays down his own importance*. John the Baptist is an excellent example of this:

> They came to John and said to him, "Rabbi, that man [Jesus—author's comment] who was with you on the other side of the Jordan—the one you testified about—well, he is baptizing and everyone is going to him." To this John replied. . ."He must become **greater**; I must become **less.**" (John 3:26, 30, NIV, bold type added)

A true prophet of God *does not try to control others* but serves others with great humility.

> Jesus called them together and said, "You know that the rulers of the Gentiles lord it over them, and their high officials exercise authority over them. Not so with you. Instead, whoever wants to become great among you must be your servant and whoever wants to be first must be your slave." (Matthew 20:25, NIV)

If the so-called prophet intimidates you so that you feel you can't walk with God without his constant "guidance" and interference, you should question whether he is really a prophet of God. If he makes you feel that he is *indispensable* to you, he is encouraging you into a *form of idolatry*.

Note also that Jeremiah 1:7-8 and 20:8-10 reveal that a prophet of God will speak what God says, even if it brings much persecution and trouble upon himself.

Possible Future Results

These false teachings, left unchallenged, will produce

many unteachable, proud so-called prophets or seers in the Church who are experts at techniques and formulas, but not in humbly discerning what God is really saying.

If these "seers" are lay people, they will generate great problems for their church leaders. If these self-appointed prophets are members of the clergy, they will damage both their lay people and their denominations. Such "seers" will cause great problems for themselves also.

These teachings need to be challenged and corrected before they produce such bad fruit.

Instead of self-appointed seers and prophets, the Church. is in need of more humble leaders and lay people who are open to hear what God is saying to them by *whatever means He chooses.*

Many of us are like Samuel. At first, Samuel did not know how to recognize God's voice (see 1 Samuel 3:2-14). Then he learned to be sensitive to God's speaking in whatever way He chose.

14
God Decides

The following verses are examples of Scriptures which reveal that God is the One who decides whether or not to give us a supernatural dream or a vision. These verses make no mention of our having to learn some techniques or formulas which will produce such revelations.

*And he said, "Hear now my words: If there be a prophet among you, **I the Lord will make myself known** unto him in a vision, and will speak unto him in a dream." (Numbers 12:6, Authorized Version, bold type added)*

__I spoke__ to the prophets, gave them many visions and told parables through them. (Hosea 12:10, NIV, bold type added)

*Then **the Lord opened Balaam's eyes**, and he saw the angel of the Lord standing in the road. . . .(Numbers 22:31, NIV, bold type added)*

The God-given dreams and visions spoken of in the Scriptures *require no prayer or spiritual growth or increased devotion to God as preparation* for receiving them. Even wicked unbelievers have received God-given dreams and visions.

A case in point: King Belshazzar of Babylon. He committed terrible sins by drinking from the sacred goblets stolen from God's Temple in Jerusalem and by praising the pagan gods of gold, silver, bronze, iron, wood and stone (see Daniel 5:22-23). The prophet Daniel stated that Belshazzar did not honor God at all (see 5:23). The king did not beseech God for a vision from Him, nor was he in a worshipful or prayerful frame of mind. Yet God chose to give him one (5:5). If we falsely believe that visions result from following certain techniques, we could wrongly assume from Daniel 5:22-24 that the more we sin, the more likely God will grant us a vision.

And Belshazzar had no trouble recognizing that this was a revelation (see Daniel 5:6). He saw the vision so clearly that his face turned pale, his knees knocked together, and his legs gave way. Belshazzar had not attended "a school of the prophets" to learn techniques of "vision viewing". God opened his spiritual eyes so he could see this sight, *regardless of whether or not he wanted to see God's revelation.*

Similarly, God spoke to an Egyptian Pharoah in two dreams (see Genesis 41:1-7), despite the fact that this pagan king believed in consulting satanic magicians and occultists (see Genesis 41:8).

God also spoke in a dream to Laban, the father of Jacob's two wives (see Genesis 31:24); despite the fact that Laban was an idol-worshipper who possibly practiced occultic divination[1] (see Genesis 31:19, 30).

These examples reveal that no spiritual preparation is required in order to receive a God-given vision or a dream. Either God decides to give you one or more, or He does not. We cannot turn supernatural dreams and visions on and off like a television set.

Effects of Prayer, Praise, Worship and Fasting

One should be commended for much prayer, praise,

worship, and other activities that tend to deepen our relationship with God. We must not be fooled, however, into thinking that such practices will increase the likelihood of His giving us greater numbers of supernatural visions and dreams.

Verses such as Acts 13:2 infer that worshipping God, fasting, prayer and praise can prepare our hearts for receiving guidance:

> *While they were worshipping the Lord and fasting, the* **Holy Spirit said**. . . . *(NIV, bold type added)*

Prayer, praise, worship and similar activities *increase the sensitivity* of our minds and spirits to hearing God speak to us. Such practices are especially invaluable to our becoming more sensitive to the witness of the Holy Spirit (see Romans 8:16) and the still small voice or inner voice of the Holy Spirit (see 1 Kings 19:12).[2]

To imply, however, that I can pressure God into constantly giving me dreams and visions by spending more time in worshipping Him, fasting, prayer and praising Him is totally unscriptural. Such an inference changes these godly practices into *means of attempting to manipulate God*, instead of avenues of intimacy with Him.

It is up to God to decide whether He will speak to us by the witness of the Spirit, the inner voice of the Holy Spirit, a God-given dream or vision, an angel, or by some other means when we are praying, praising and worshipping Him.

Note also: the Scriptures reveal that God does not only speak to us when we are praying and fasting, worshipping Him, or praising Him. God spoke to Moses in the desert

---

[1]Depending on whether we translate the Hebrew word *nachash*, in Genesis 30:27, as being "divination" or "experience".

[2]Refer to my book *How To Recognize God's Voice* for more details of these two ways God speaks to us.

of Midian when he apparently was not doing any of these things (see Exodus 3:1-6). He tried to communicate with Samuel at a time when he was neither recorded as praying, worshipping nor praising God (see 1 Samuel 3:1-9).

A Qualifying Point

It is possible to argue that if a person does not pray and wait on God often, he will not be spiritually sensitive enough to know when God is giving him one of the third category-types of God-given visions, mentioned in Chapter 2. This category of God-given visions does not involve His suspending the physical senses or His revealing the spiritual realm through the person's physical eyes. Instead, they are merely visual impressions in the person's mind.

To argue this, however, is different from suggesting wrongly that the more we look for God-given visions and dreams, the more of these He will send us.

15
Exceptions Don't Make Rules

Someone may argue: "According to 2 Kings 6:16-17, God honored Elisha's request by granting his servant a supernatural vision. Surely this reveals that God will always or customarily give a vision or dream to those Christians who persistently ask Him for one."

This argument is wrong for several reasons:

Only 1.6 Percent

First, when we examine the Scriptures closely we find that all of the 21 recorded instances of God-given dreams (that I know of) were given without there being any mention of someone's asking Him to grant them.[1]

I also find in the Scriptures 40 incidents of God-given visions.[2] Of these, *only one* was requested. Therefore, out of 61 God-given dreams and visions recorded in the

---

[1]Genesis 20:3-7; 28:12; 31:10-13, 24; 37:5-8, 9-11; 40:5-19 (two dreams together here); 41:1, 5; Judges 7:13-15; 1 Kings 3:5-15; Daniel 2:1; 4:5; 7:1; Matthew 1:20; 2:12, 13, 19-20, 22; 27:19.

[2]Genesis 15:1; 18:1-2; 21:19; 46:2-4; Exodus 3:1-6; 16:10; Numbers 24:4; Joshua 5:13-15; 1 Samuel 3:2-15; 2 Kings 6:16-17; Isaiah 1:1; 6:1-13; 21:2; Ezekiel 1:1; 3:14-15; 8:1-11:25; 37:1-14; 40:1-48:35; Daniel 2:19; 7:1-15; 8:1-14; 10:1-12:13; Obadiah 1:1-21; Nahum 1:1-3:19; Zechariah 1:8-6:15; Matthew 17:1-5; Luke 1:11-22; 24:23; Acts 7:55-56; 9:1-8; 9:10-11; 9:12; 10:1-6; 10:9-20; 16:9-10; 18:9-10; 22:17-18; 23:11; 2 Corinthians 12:1-4; and Revelation 1:10-22:17.

Scriptures, *only 1.6 percent* came as a result of someone's request. Such a small percentage infers to me that only on *rare* occasions will God grant a vision or a dream to someone who specifically asks for one.

No Unambiguous Promise

Secondly, note that there is no clear-cut promise recorded in the Scriptures that God will give a supernatural dream or vision, angelic visitation, or supernatural sign to every person who asks for one.

One Exception
Does Not Create a Biblical Rule

Thirdly, when we compare the example recorded in 2 Kings 6:16-17 to the frequency with which God grants angelic appearances, we find that one exception does not provide us with a biblical rule of how He will always or mostly respond to such requests.

It's true that God granted Manoah's request and returned His angel (see Judges 13:2-11). But when we examine the other 42 references in Scripture where God enabled persons to see angels and/or hear them speak, we find that nowhere is it recorded that these were requested by those who received them.[3]

---

[3]Genesis 16:7-12; 18:1-22; 21:17; 22:11-18; 28:12; 31:11; 32:1-2; Exodus 3:2; Numbers 22:22-35; Judges 2:1-4; 6:11-18; 2 Samuel 24:16-17; 1 Kings 19:5-8; 2 Kings 1:3-4; 1 Chronicles 21:9-30; Daniel 6:21-22; 8:16-26; 9:21-23; Zechariah 1:8-21; 2:3-5; 4:1-5;5:5-11; 6:1-8; Matthew 1:20-24; 2:13-15; 2:19-21; 4:11; 28:2-7; Mark 1:13; Luke 1:11-22; 1:26-38; 2:9-12; 2:13-15; 22:43; 24:23; John 20:11-13; Acts 5:19-20; 8:26; 10:3-7; 12:6-11; 27:23-25, and the many angels seen by the Apostle John, as recorded in the Book of Revelation.

It is possible that some of these angelic appearances or visitations were christophanies. A christophany is an appearance of God the Son in spiritual form before He was incarnated in the flesh about 2000 years ago. These possible christophanies recorded in Genesis 16:7-13; Exodus 3:2; Numbers 22:23-35, and Judges 2:1-4.

Observe that the example recorded in both 2 Kings 19:35 and 2 Chronicles 32:20-21 refers to a situation in which King Hezekiah and the prophet Isaiah asked for God's intervention. Note also that they *did not specifically request* God to send an angel (2 Kings 19:14-19 and Isaiah 36:1—37:36 tell of the same example). Neither did they actually see the angel.

In the example found in 1 Chronicles 21:9-30, it was God who gave King David a choice between three punishments—one of the options was that God would send an angel in judgment. David *did not initiate* this request. God initiated this situation *limiting* David's choices to only three.

Hebrews 13:2 is an interesting verse. It reveals that God has sent angels to people who were not even aware of it at that time.

Look closely at the example found in Judges 13:2-11. God originally sent His Angel to Manoah's wife *without anyone asking Him to do so*. Therefore, Manoah's request for the return of God's Angel was *in response* to something that *God already had initiated*.

This Manoah exception does not provide us with a biblical rule that God always or generally will grant an angelic appearance to those who ask for one.

A fair comparison is the example found in Joshua 10:1-14, where God miraculously stopped the sun from moving across the sky in answer to Joshua's request. We would be foolish to suggest that this single biblical example gives every believer the right to expect the sun to stand still upon request. Joshua 10:13-14 reveals that such events are rare occurrences:

> . . .*The sun stopped in the middle of the sky and delayed going down about a full day. There has never been a day like it before or since, a day when the Lord listened to a man. . . . (NIV)*

The writer of the Book of Joshua knew of no other examples of this before or after this event up until the time of the author's death.

Other than the events recorded in 2 Kings 20:9-11, in which the sun went backwards across the sky, how many examples do you know of where the sun stopped or changed its course in answer to prayer?

God Accommodated Himself

Fourthly, a study of 2 Kings 6:6-17, shows in this example that God accommodated Himself to the weakness of Elisha's servant. Elisha did not ask for a God-given vision for himself. His words, *"Those who are with us are more than those who are with them,"* reveal two possibilities: either Elisha had faith that God's promises about angelic protection, such as those spoken previously by the prophet David (see Psalm 91:11-12), were true; or God, in His sovereignty, previously had shown these angelic protectors to Elisha.

Whatever the case, Elisha asked for the God-given vision for his servant and not for himself. The wording of 2 Kings 6:17 reveals this:

> . . .*O Lord, open **his** eyes so **he** may see. (NIV, bold type added)*

Elisha's words, *"Don't be afraid,"* reveal that his servant was tempted to be frightened at the time. So, in great mercy, God provided sensory proof of His protection to Elisha's servant by granting him the vision.

When saying that God accommodates Himself to human weakness on rare occasions, I'm not suggesting that God ever lowers Himself to participate in or approve of human

100

sin. Instead, I'm saying that just as human parents will do things for their one-year-old that they won't do for their healthy, sixteen-year-old, God sometimes acts similarly towards His children depending on their spiritual maturity.

Also, I'm defining human weakness as being something different from sin. For example, all human minds are weak in comparison to God's mind. This weakness of the human mind may lead to sin, but is not sin itself.

Because Elisha often had seen God's miraculous power and love for him in action, God may have regarded as unacceptable any request by the prophet for physical evidence of God's protection for himself. He may have considered such a request as indication of a lack of faith.

Remember that Jesus regarded the Apostle Thomas' insistence on physical proof of Jesus Christ's resurrection from the dead as being a sign of the sin of unbelief. Jesus said to Thomas: ". . .*Put your finger here; see my hands. Reach out your hand and put it into my side.* **Stop doubting** *and believe"* (John 20:27, NIV, bold type added).

Jesus went on to say to Thomas: ". . .*Because you have seen me, you have believed; blessed are those who have not seen and yet have believed"* (John 20:29, NIV).

This is not to say that all those who receive God-given visions and dreams have much unbelief. It does, however, mean that a request for a vision or dream for ourselves may indicate, in many instances, a lack of faith and our need for sensory proof before we will trust God about something.

Old Testament Exceptions

Not only is there a biblical example of God accommodating Himself to the weakness of a person by granting

101

him a requested vision, the Old Testament contains a few examples of God accommodating Himself to the weaknesses of believers by granting their requests for specific signs in their circumstances. Three such examples are recorded in Genesis 24:10-27, Judges 6:36-40, and 1 Samuel 14:4-15. In these instances, God answered their requests by giving them the specific signs they requested.

But note that the Scriptures contain no promise that God will give us the specific sign we may request. Therefore, we cannot use the above three examples to suggest that He will mostly grant such requests.

We must remember that in Old Testament times, only a few believers were given the Holy Spirit. These were the prophets, some of the leaders of Israel and Bezalel, the craftsman who worked on the Old Testament Tabernacle (see Exodus 31:1-11). Even these people did not have the Holy Spirit in the same way that a born-again believer would in New Testament times (see John 7:39, Ezekiel 36:22-29). Consequently, in Old Testament times God sometimes used external forms of guidance which He no longer uses.

During the years that Moses and the people of Israel were in the desert, God guided them by a pillar of cloud by day and a pillar of fire at night (see Exodus 13:21-22; Numbers 14:14; Nehemiah 9:12, 19). On occasion, God also used the Urim and Thummin to guide the people of Israel. We are not sure what these were, but they were worn on the breast of the High Priest's clothes (see Exodus 28:15-30). In the New Testament, the Urim and Thummin are not mentioned as means God uses anymore to guide His people.

In Old Testament times, God also allowed the high priests and leaders of Israel to use the casting of lots sometimes to discover His will. Verses such as Leviticus 16:8-10, Numbers 34:13-17, Joshua 21:1-4, 1 Samuel 14:36-42,

1 Chronicles 24:2-5 and Nehemiah 10:34 taken together seem to infer that the lots were kept in the possession of the high priests. Proverbs 16:33 reveals that God sanctioned this *external* method of guidance. One possibility is that the lots and the Urim and Thummin worn by the High Priest were the same thing.

The Apostles tried to use this method of guidance (see Acts 1:21-26). But note that they are not recorded as having used lots after they received the Holy Spirit on the Day of Pentecost. Since none of the Apostles was a high priest and the Scriptures do not say that God approved of their selection of Matthias as the apostolic replacement for Judas Iscariot, it is likely that their use of the lots was not sanctioned by God. Some suggest that Paul was God's choice to replace Judas (see Galatians 2:7-9).[4]

The New Testament makes it clear that after the death and resurrection of the Lord Jesus, the Father desires to guide His people primarily by His Scriptures (see 2 Timothy 3:16; 2 Peter 1:20-21), secondly by the guidance of His Holy Spirit (see John 16:13; 10:27), thirdly by whatever sign in our circumstances He chooses to give, and fourthly, but more rarely, by dreams or other more spectacular forms of guidance. (Refer to my book *How To Recognize God's Voice* for more details.)

Genesis 24:10-27 reveals that in great kindness and mercy, God gave Abraham's servant the sign in his circumstances he requested. There is no mention in the Bible of Abraham's servant having the Holy Spirit. The

---

[4]The *only use* of lots authorized by the Sacred Scriptures was in Old Testament times by the high priests and the leaders of Israel. There is not one unambiguous verse in the New Testament which states that God wishes born-of-the-Holy-Spirit Christians to use lots as a form of guidance. Also, nowhere in the Book of Acts or other books of the New Testament does it say that God approved of the Apostles naively using this method of guidance.

Note also that in ancient times, pagans had their own demonic, occultic form of casting of lots (see Esther 3:7; Obadiah 11; Nahum 3:10; and Matthew 27:35). Therefore, if a Christian attempts to use lots as a means of guidance, he leaves himself open to demonic deception.

Urim and Thummin were not in existence then. Also, Abraham's servant did not have a prophet of God with him at the time to give him God's guidance. (In Old Testament times, God approved of people going to His prophets to obtain His guidance. In New Testament times, however, God wishes to guide us primarily by His Scriptures and His Holy Spirit, even though His prophets may confirm to us what His Holy Spirit has already said to us—See Acts 20:22-23 and Acts 21:10-13 taken together.) Therefore, as an *exception*, God revealed His will by giving Abraham's servant the sign he requested.

Although Abraham's servant obviously had some sort of relationship with God (see Genesis 24:26), it did not seem to be a strong personal relationship. This is seen when three times, the servant addressed God as "*O Lord, the God of my master Abraham*," instead of as "O Lord, my God" (see Genesis 24:12, 27 and 42). This would be like me calling God "O Lord, the God of my mother". Such an expression would infer that I lacked intimacy with Him.

God *accommodated* Himself to the relative spiritual weakness of Abraham's servant by granting his request for a sign. Genesis 24:45 reveals that God arranged for Rebekah to be heading to the exact place at the exact time Abraham's servant would be asking Him to send the wife that He had planned for Isaac. Such fore-planning by God shows how keen He was to accommodate Himself to the servant's lack of intimacy with His Holy Spirit.

Let us compare this to Abraham. Abraham was a prophet (see Genesis 20:7) and therefore was intimate with God the Holy Spirit. Abraham did not ask God for specific signs in his circumstances.

In the second example, recorded in Judges 6:36-40, we see that God gave Gideon the two signs he requested. But note God did this as an exception also.

Note that God previously had revealed His will to Gideon about the matter (see Judges 6:11-16). God disclosed His will through the words of His angel and by giving Gideon a specific sign that He wished to give.

Gideon began his request for the first sign with, *"If you will save Israel by my hand **as you have promised**. . ."* (see Judges 6:36, bold type added). This expression reveals that Gideon already knew God's will when he asked for the sign.

Gideon asked for these signs because of *his lack of faith* in God's faithfulness and power to fulfil His promise. Gideon was testing God by asking for these signs when God already had promised clearly to help. Gideon's words in Judges 6:39, *"Do not be angry with me,"* reveal that even Gideon knew he was testing God by asking for specific signs. In Matthew 12:38-39, we see that Jesus rebuked the Pharisees for testing Him by their asking for more miraculous signs than He had already given.

Gideon expressed also a lack of understanding of God's dealings, a trust in self instead of God and a fear of people (see Judges 6:13-15, 27). But because of His great love for the oppressed Israelites, God accommodated Himself to Gideon's weakness and gave the two requested signs.

It is little wonder that as an exception, God did this for Gideon. Later in Judges 8:22-27, we see how spiritually inconsistent Gideon was. First, when asked to be the ruler of Israel, he said rightly that the Lord should be their ruler, not him or his sons. Then immediately after, he made an idol of gold. This was a terrible sin. He seemed to have no understanding that previously, God had commanded all Israelites to never make idols (see Exodus 20:4-5).

In the third example recorded in 1 Samuel 14:4-15, we see that Jonathan, King Saul's son asked God to give him a specific sign. Note, however, that Jonathan did not have the Holy Spirit. Also, in this instance, he did not take with him to the pass a prophet of God or a high priest wearing an ephod containing the Urim and Thummin. As a result, Jonathan was cut off from the normal sources of God's guidance at that time. Therefore in great mercy and kindness, God accommodated Himself to Jonathan's weakness, granting him the requested sign. Observe also that Jonathan's use of the word *perhaps* (see 1 Samuel 14:6) reveals that he was not sure God would grant his request for a sign.

Note that Hannah's prayer for a son (see 1 Samuel 1:10-11) was not a request for a sign, but was a request accompanied by a vow. Also, observe that in the instance of God granting King Hezekiah a sign through the prophet Isaiah (see 2 Kings 20:8-11), Hezekiah did not ask for a specific sign at first. Hezekiah only requested a specific sign after God through Isaiah gave him a choice between two miraculous signs (see 2 Kings 20:9-10; Isaiah 38:4-8).

It is possible even in New Testament times that God may accommodate Himself to the weakness of a Christian, who does not know better, by granting him/her a requested specific sign. But this is no excuse for a Christian, who knows better, to try to take advantage of God's graciousness by asking for specific signs.

Personal Examples

In one isolated instance in my own life, God granted me a supernatural dream after I had asked Him to do so. Before drawing any rash conclusion, consider the circumstances:

For many months, I had been asking God what to do about a specific, tormenting problem. On the basis of James 1:5, I asked God for wisdom, knowing that He would give it. Yet, I did not request the guidance to be given by any particular means.

One morning, just before I awoke, the Lord gave me a supernatural dream in which He spoke three words to me. I awoke and began to wonder what this dream meant. Finally, I sought an interpretation to the dream by asking the Lord to give me another dream. In great mercy, He answered my request and gave me a second dream the next day just before I awoke.

Note that my request for a second dream was in response to something *God already had initiated.* Observe also that there is no verse of Scripture which says unequivocally that God will always grant a dream or a vision to someone who asks for it.

Once when I tried to follow the example of Gideon and Abraham's servant by asking for a specific miraculous sign in my circumstances, God *refused to answer.* I prayed, "Lord, if You will for me to marry Rita (who later became my wife), lead her to talk to me and take interest in me after our special Saturday night church meetings over the next few weeks." Even though He revealed later, *in ways that He chose,* that it was His will for her to marry me, God did not bring this miraculous sign about.

I unwisely expected God to give me this sign, when there is no verse of Scripture clearly promising that God will always answer requests for specific forms of guidance.

Summary

In this New Testament age, God can accommodate Himself on occasion to a human's weakness by granting that person a supernatural dream, vision, sign in his circumstances, or angelic appearance upon request. To suggest, however, that God always, or as a rule, grants these things to us as a result of our constantly seeking after them, is contrary to the Scriptures taken as a whole.

Conclusion

The Scriptures reveal that God wishes to speak sometimes via dreams and visions. Note, however, that God-given dreams and visions will occur in our lives only if He wishes to speak to us in these specific ways. He is the Lord over how He will address us. We are not the lord of this. Let us allow God to be God.

If we try to force God into doing things that He knows is not right for us at the time, we will not be Holy Spirit-controlled Christians.

We need to learn the differences between different types of dreams and visions. If we don't, we are in danger of being very confused if we are granted one.

We must also learn how to use our God-given imagination in ways that are in agreement with the Scriptures and guided by the Holy Spirit.

If we have a dream or a vision that we think is from God, we should test it to see if it is really from Him. Similarly, if someone else states that God has given him a dream or vision for us, we should test it by the Scriptures and by seeing if the Holy Spirit confirms to us the same message.

If God has foreordained a person to be a prophet or seer, this is good. But I pity those who take the mantle of a prophet upon themselves without God wanting this.

Visions and dreams from God are wonderful things. But beware of Satanic and fleshly substitutes.

If you have enjoyed this book and would like to help us to send a copy of it and many other titles to needy pastors in the **Third World**, please write for further information or send your gift to:

Sovereign World Trust, P.O. Box 777, Tonbridge, Kent TN11 9XT, United Kingdom

or to the **'Sovereign World'** distributor in your country. If sending money from outside the United Kingdom, please send an International Money Order or Foreign Bank Draft in STERLING, drawn on a **UK** bank to **Sovereign World Trust**.